The Primitive Edge
of Experience

Other Books by Thomas H. Ogden

The Primitive Edge of Experience

Thomas H. Ogden, M.D.

Jason Aronson Inc.
Northvale, New Jersey
London

Certain chapters in this book are based on prior publications of the author. He gratefully acknowledges permission from the following journals to reprint this previously published material.

Chapter 2: "On the dialectical structure of experience: some clinical and theoretical implications," *Contemporary Psychoanalysis* 24:17–45, 1988 (copyright © W. A. White Institute). This paper was originally written as a contribution to *Master Clinicians on Treating the Regressed Patient,* ed. L. B. Boyer and P. L. Giovacchini. Northvale, NJ: Jason Aronson, 1989.

Chapter 3: "On the concept of an autistic-contiguous position," *The International Journal of Psycho-Analysis* 70:127–140, 1989 (copyright © Institute of Psycho-Analysis).

Chapter 5: "The transitional Oedipal relationship in female development," *The International Journal of Psycho-Analysis* 68:485–498, 1987 (copyright © Institute of Psycho-Analysis).

Chapter 6: "The threshold of the male Oedipus complex," *The Bulletin of the Menninger Clinic* 53:394–413, 1989 (copyright © The Menninger Foundation).

Chapter 8: "Misrecognitions and the fear of not knowing," *The Psychoanalytic Quarterly* 57:643–666, 1988 (copyright © The Psychoanalytic Quarterly, Inc.).

Jason Aronson Inc. gratefully acknowledges permission from New Directions Publishing Corporation to reprint an excerpt from *Labyrinths* by Jorge Luis Borges. Copyright © 1962, 1964 by New Directions Publishing Corporation. The publisher also gratefully acknowledges permission from Harcourt Brace, Jovanovich, Inc. to reprint excerpts from *Four Quartets.* Copyright © 1943 by T. S. Eliot and renewed 1971 by Esme Valerie Eliot.

Library of Congress Cataloging-in-Publication Data

Ogden, Thomas H.
    The primitive edge of experience   Thomas H. Ogden.
        p.   cm.
    Bibliography: p.
    Includes index.
    ISBN 0-87668-982-9
    1. Psychoanalysis.   I. Title.
    RC506.034   1989   89-6878
    616.89'17 — dc20   CIP

Manufactured in the United States of America. Jason Aronson Inc. offers books and cassettes. For information and catalog write to Jason Aronson Inc., 230 Livingston Street, Northvale, New Jersey 07647.

For my sons
Pete and Ben,
with love

Contents

1

Introduction 1

2

The Structure of Experience 9

3

The Autistic-Contiguous Position 47

4

The Schizoid Condition 83

5

The Transitional Oedipal Relationship in Female Development 109

6

The Threshold of the Male Oedipus Complex 141

7

The Initial Analytic Meeting 169

8

Misrecognitions and the Fear of Not Knowing 195

1

Introduction

This book, having been written, has become part of the given and must now be overcome in the minds of its readers and its author. Having been written, it is static and no longer becoming anything other than itself. The potential value of this book lies in the degree to which it creates a possibility for the given (of which it is now a part) to be overcome through interpretation by the reader in a new and more generative way.

As analysts, we attempt to assist the analysand in his efforts at freeing himself from forms of organized experience (his conscious and unconscious "knowledge" of himself) that entrap him and prevent him from tolerating the experience of not knowing long enough to create understandings in a different way. The value of developing new ways of knowing lies not simply in the greater self-understanding one might achieve, but as importantly in the possibility that a wider range of thoughts, feelings, and sensations might be brought into being. Each insight, however valuable, immediately constitutes the next resistance in that the new knowledge is already part of the static known and must be overcome in the process of freshly knowing.

1

It is necessary that both the analytic discourse between analysts and the analytic dialogue between analyst and analysand serve as "containers" for the experience of confusion and not knowing. If all is going well in the analytic process, the analysand will inevitably complain that he understands even less at present than he did at the beginning of the analysis. (More accurately, he understands less than he *thought* he knew at the outset of the analysis, and he is learning to tolerate not knowing.)

A reader, like an analysand, dares to experience the disturbing feeling of not knowing each time he begins reading a new piece of writing. We regularly create the soothing illusion for ourselves that we have nothing to lose from the experience of reading, and that we can only gain from it. This rationalization is superficial salve for the wound that we are about to open in the process of our effort to learn. In attempting to learn, we subject ourselves to the tension of dissolving the connections between ideas that we have thus far relied upon in a particular way: What we think we know helps us identify who we are (or more accurately, who we think we are).

Reading a psychoanalytic book is a particularly difficult undertaking in that the reader has chosen to attempt to learn about a body of ideas (and a therapeutic process) in which a principal focus is on that which cannot be known: the unconscious mind. The unconscious is by definition unknowable in that once the individual has become aware of a given thought, feeling, phantasy, sensation, or the like, it is no longer an aspect of unconscious experience. The psychoanalyst is therefore in the unfortunate position of being a student of that which cannot be known. It is little wonder that we cling to our ideologies, our patriarchs and matriarchs, our analytic heroes and heretics, and our analytic schools, all of which serve us in our efforts to avoid awareness of our confusion.

The Oedipus myth, so fundamental to the psychoanalytic conception of the human dilemma, is an endlessly twisting labyrinth revolving around the question of whether it is better to know or not to know, better to be known or not to be known. If Oedipus had known that the man with whom he entered into battle on the road from Delphi was his own father, would he have done otherwise? The question, of course, is moot — it could not have been otherwise. One cannot know these things; the idea that it is possible to know them is mere self-deception. Oedipus's eventual knowledge of his dual crime brought with it resolution and disaster of equal magnitude. Would it have been better not to have known? Even after having recognized the truth of Teiresias's words, Oedipus knew, but could not bear to know (see) what he saw.

Not knowing deprives us of our sense of who we are, and yet to know is to see that which we cannot bear to see. The analysand desperately darts between wishes to know and wishes not to know. Similarly, it is our need to know that leads us to read; at the same time, we are deterred from reading by our unconscious knowledge that the book that we are about to read (if it is worth reading) will plunge us into the experience of feeling that we know even less than we thought we did, and will lead us to feel that we know ourselves even less well than we had thought.

To a large extent, this book is concerned with the primitive edge of human experience, the ". . . frontiers of consciousness beyond which words fail though meanings still exist" (T. S. Eliot, 1950).

The history of the development of British object

relations theory over the past twenty years can be viewed as containing the beginnings of the exploration of an area of human experience that lies beyond the psychological states addressed by Klein's concept of the paranoid–schizoid and the depressive positions; by Fairbairn's conception of the world of unconscious internal object relations; by Bion's conception of projective identification as a form of object relatedness and communication; or by Winnicott's conception of the early mother–infant unit. I shall introduce the concept of an autistic-contiguous position as a way of conceiving of the most primitive psychological organization through which the sensory "floor" of the experience of self is generated.

The autistic-contiguous position is understood as a sensory-dominated, presymbolic area of experience in which the most primitive form of meaning is generated on the basis of the organization of sensory impressions, particularly at the skin surface. A unique form of anxiety arises in this psychological realm: terror over the prospect that the boundedness of one's sensory surface might be dissolved, with a resultant feeling of falling, leaking, dropping, into an endless and shapeless space.

I explore in this book the idea that human experience is the product of the dialectical interplay of three modes of generating experience: the depressive, the paranoid-schizoid, and the autistic-contiguous. Each mode creates, preserves, and negates the other. Just as the idea of the conscious mind has no meaning independent of the idea of the unconscious mind, no single mode of generating experience exists independently of the others. Each is the negating context for the other.

From this perspective, psychopathology is conceptualized as a collapse of the dialectic in the direction of one or the other of the modes of generating experience. The

outcome of such a collapse may be a tyrannizing entrapment in rigid, asymbolic patternings of sensation (collapse in the direction of the autistic-contiguous mode); or
imprisonment in a world of omnipotent internal objects
wherein thoughts and feelings are experienced as things
and forces (collapse in the direction of the paranoid-
schizoid mode); or the isolation of the self from the
immediacy of lived experience and the aliveness of bodily
sensations (collapse in the direction of the depressive
mode).

On the basis of the ideas thus summarized, I con-
clude that a revised conception of the schizoid condition is
required. No longer is it adequate to generate understandings of schizoid phenomena based on a view that
Klein's paranoid-schizoid position or Fairbairn's internal
object world represents the most primitive psychological
organizations. The autistic-contiguous position is viewed
as the "underbelly" or primitive edge of the schizoid
personality organization. I propose that schizoid experience is generated in an area of experience lying between
the realm of strangulated internal object relations and
the realm of tyrannizing, asymbolic patternings of sensation. Through discussing certain aspects of the analysis
of a schizoid patient, I attempt to illustrate the ways in
which analytic theory and technique must incorporate an
understanding of the nature of the interplay of autistic-
contiguous, paranoid-schizoid, and depressive modes of
generating experience.

In Chapters 5 and 6, the focus of the discussion
shifts to an examination of the transition into the Oedipus
complex in female and male development. Since there is
no assumption of symmetry between male and female
development, the transitions into the male and female
Oedipus complex are addressed separately.

Although the Oedipus complex has been from the beginning one of the cornerstones of the psychoanalytic edifice, the psychological-interpersonal processes mediating the transition into the Oedipus complex have remained obscure. In part, this is a reflection of the fact that, until relatively recently, analytic theory has failed to adequately conceptualize the distinction between pre-Oedipal and Oedipal object relations; moreover, there has been a paucity of analytic concepts that address the interplay of intrapsychic and interpersonal realms of experience.

The concept of a transitional Oedipal relationship is proposed as a way of understanding the psychological-interpersonal processes mediating the entry into the female Oedipus complex. As is the case with other transitional phenomena, this transitional relationship serves the function of allowing the discovery of otherness in a form that is experienced as both *me* and *not-me* at the same time. In the context of the transitional relationship created by mother and daughter at the threshold of the Oedipus complex, the little girl falls in love with her mother who is unconsciously identified with her own (internal object) Oedipal father. The question of whether the little girl is in love with her mother or father (in love with an internal object or an external object) never arises.

By means of this transitional relationship, the little girl nontraumatically discovers the externality of the Oedipal father (and mother) in the context of the safety of a dyadic relationship with the pre-Oedipal mother. As a result, paradoxically, the first heterosexual love relationship unfolds in the context of a relationship involving two females; the initial triangulation of object relations occurs within a dyadic relationship.

It is necessary to generate an understanding of the

transition into the Oedipus complex that is specific to male development, an understanding that is not simply a transposition of one's conception of the entry into the female Oedipus complex. The transition into the male Oedipus complex differs from the transition into the female Oedipus complex in that, for the male, there is no "change of object." That is, for the boy, the mother is the object of both pre-Oedipal attachment to an omnipotent internal object and Oedipal desire for an external whole object.

I view the psychological-interpersonal movement into triangulated Oedipal object relations as mediated for the boy by the elaboration of mature forms of the primal scene phantasy, in conjunction with the development of a type of transitional Oedipal relationship to the mother that is distinctive to male development. In the transitional Oedipal relationship in male development, the mother is both the (internal object) mother and the (external object) father (through whom the little boy is empowered phallically). The actual father is only secondarily the bearer of the phallus.

I then turn in Chapter 7 to a discussion of early experience of a different sort: the beginnings of the analytic experience. The analyst must allow himself to be freshly surprised by the ideas and phenomena that he takes most for granted. In this chapter, I attempt to re-approach the initial analytic meeting as if for the first time.

In this discussion, I view the initial face-to-face analytic meeting as not simply a preparation for the analysis, but as the actual beginning of the analysis. I propose the notion that, in the initial meeting, the analyst listens for the patient's "cautionary tales" — that is, for the patient's unconscious warnings to the analyst and to himself regarding his reasons for feeling that the analysis is a dangerous and doomed undertaking. Whatever the nature of the patient's psychological difficulties, his unconscious anxiety will be given form in terms of the danger he experiences in relation to the prospect of beginning analysis. The analyst attempts to understand the nature of these transference anxieties and to help the analysand put these fears into words.

In the final chapter, I discuss a specific form of primitive anxiety: the unconscious fear of not knowing. What the individual is not able to know is what he feels — and therefore who, if anyone, he is. The terror associated with this type of not knowing is warded off by means of the use of substitute formations (misnamings and misrecognitions) that create for the individual the illusion of knowing and of being. Defensive reliance on substitute formations further alienates the individual from himself, and fills the potential space in which personal meaning and desire might otherwise have come into being.

This type of fear of not knowing is by no means restricted to a small group of alexithymic or schizoid patients. It is a universal phenomenon, one that, to some degree, we continually bump up against; it is experienced, for example, each time we expose ourselves to the hazards of learning.

2

The Structure of Experience

> *The other one, the one called Borges, is
> the one things happen to . . . I know of
> Borges from the mail . . . It would be
> an exaggeration to say that ours is a
> hostile relationship; I live it, let myself
> go on living, so that Borges may contrive
> his literature, and this literature justifies
> me.*
>
> J. L. Borges, "Borges and I"

Borges's prose poem "Borges and I" (1960) delicately
teases apart what ordinarily comprises the illusion of
unity of experience. In an infinitely more clumsy way I
would like to propose a psychoanalytic framework within
which to think about the components of the dialectical
process generating human experience. I will explore in
this chapter the idea that human experience is constituted
by the dialectical interplay of three different modes of
generating experience: the depressive mode, the paranoid-
schizoid mode, and the autistic-contiguous mode. The

9

concept of the first two of these modes was introduced by
Melanie Klein[1]; the third represents my own synthesis,
clarification, and extension of ideas introduced primarily
by Frances Tustin, Esther Bick, and Donald Meltzer.
Each of these modes of generating experience is characterized by its own form of symbolization, method of
defense, quality of object relatedness, and degree of
subjectivity. The three modes stand in a dialectical
relationship to one another, each creating, preserving,
and negating the others. The idea of a single mode
functioning without relation to the other two is as meaningless as the concept of the conscious mind in isolation
from the concept of the unconscious mind; each is an
empty set filled by the other pole or poles of the dialectic.

I will describe each of the three modes of generating
experience with particular reference to the analytic experience. What I hope will become apparent is that every
psychological event is overdetermined, not only in terms
of layers of unconscious content, but also in terms of
modes of experience generating the psychological matrix
within which mental content exists. Psychological change
("structural change") will be discussed in terms of shifts in
the nature of the dialectical interplay of modes of generating experience.

Paradoxically, the elements of the synchronicity of
experience will, for the sake of clarity, be presented

---

[1]Although I am not a Kleinian, I have found many of Klein's ideas —
when viewed independently of her developmental timetable, her
concept of the death instinct, and her theory of technique — to be
pivotal to the development of psychoanalytic thought. Two of her
most important contributions to psychoanalysis are the concepts of
the paranoid-schizoid and depressive positions. However, neither
concept has been integrated into the main body of the American
psychoanalytic dialogue.

sequentially in this chapter. Like a novice juggler who requires the patience of his audience while he gets his first baton into solitary flight, I ask for the reader's indulgence while I launch the initial sections of this chapter. In the end, the reader must become the juggler holding in generative tension the multiplicity of modes constituting human experience.

Experience in a Depressive Mode

The concept of the *depressive* position was introduced by Melanie Klein (1935, 1948, 1958) to refer to the most mature form of psychological organization. Although this organization continues to develop throughout life, Klein believed that it has its origins in the second quarter of the first year of life.[2] Bion (1962) modified this concept to emphasize not its place in a developmental sequence, but its place in a dynamic relationship with the paranoid-schizoid position. In this chapter, my focus is on the depressive mode not as a structure or a developmental phase, but as a process through which perception is attributed meaning in a particular way. This is what I have in mind by a mode of generating experience. The qualities of experience in each mode are interdependent, each providing the context for the other.

In the depressive position, the mode of symbolization termed *symbol formation proper* (Segal, 1957) is one in which the symbol re-presents the symbolized and is experienced as different from it. Symbolic meaning is

---

[2]As will be seen, the debate over Klein's developmental timetable loses much of its significance when her "positions" are viewed not as developmental phases, but as synchronic dimensions of experience.

generated by a subject mediating between the symbol and that which it represents. It could be said that it is in the space between the symbol and the symbolized that an interpreting subject comes into being. It could also be said with equal validity that it is the development of the capacity for subjectivity, the experience of "I-ness," however subtle and unobtrusive, that makes it possible for the individual to mediate between symbol and symbolized. Both are true. Each constitutes the conditions necessary for the other; neither "leads to" or "causes" the other in a linear, sequential sense.

The achievement of symbol formation proper allows one to experience oneself as a person thinking one's thoughts and feeling one's feelings. In this way, thoughts and feelings are experienced to a large degree as personal creations that can be understood (interpreted). Thus, for better or for worse, one develops a feeling of responsibility for one's psychological actions (thoughts, feelings, and behavior).

As one becomes capable of experiencing oneself as a subject, one at the same time (via projection and identification) becomes capable of experiencing one's "objects" as also being subjects. That is, other people are viewed as being alive and capable of thinking and feeling in the same way that one experiences oneself as having one's own thoughts and feelings. This is the world of whole object relations in which the individual exists as more or less the same person over time, in relation to other people who also continue to be the same people despite powerful affective shifts and mixtures of affect. New experience is added to old, but new experience does not undo or negate the past. The continuity of experience of self and other through loving and hating feeling states, is the context for the development of the capacity for ambivalence.

Historicity is created in the depressive mode as the individual relinquishes his or her reliance on omnipotent defenses. When, in a paranoid-schizoid mode, one feels disappointed or angry at an object, the object is no longer experienced as the same object that it had been, but as a new object. This experience of the discontinuity of self and object over time precludes the creation of historicity. Instead there is a continual, defensive recasting of the past. In a depressive mode, one is rooted in a history that one creates through interpreting one's past. Although one's interpretations of the past are evolving (and therefore history is continually evolving and changing), the past is understood to be immutable. This knowledge brings with it the sadness that one's past will never be all that one had wished. For example, one's early relationships with one's parents will never be all that one has hoped. At the same time, this rootedness in time also brings a depth and stability to one's experience of self. One's relation to the history that one has created interpretively is an important dimension of subjectivity, without which one's experience of "I-ness" feels arbitrary, erratic, and unreal.

In a psychological state in which other people are experienced as subjects and not simply as objects, it is possible to care about them as opposed to simply valuing them as one would value a prized object, or even such essential objects as food or air. Objects can be damaged or used up; only subjects can be hurt. Therefore, only in the context of the experience of *subjective others* does the experience of guilt become a potential human experience. Guilt has no meaning in the absence of the capacity for concern for other people as subjects. Guilt is a specific sort of pain that one bears *over time* in response to real or imagined harm that one has done to someone about whom one cares. One can attempt to make reparation for that about which one feels guilty, but this does not undo what one has done. All the individual can do is to attempt to make up for what he has done, in his subsequent relations with others and with himself. Empathy becomes possible in this mode of experience, since others are experienced as subjects whose feelings can be understood to be like one's own.

Once the other is experienced as a subject as well as an object, one acknowledges the life of the other outside the area of one's omnipotence. In a world of subjects whom one ambivalently loves and cannot fully control, a distinctly new form of anxiety (not possible in the more primitive modes of experience) is generated: the anxiety that one's anger has driven away or harmed the person one loves. Sadness, the experience of missing someone, loneliness, and the capacity for mourning become dimensions of human experience as a consequence of the interplay of the qualities of experience in the depressive mode described above. As will be discussed, in a paranoid–schizoid mode, magical restoration of the lost object short-circuits these experiences. There is no need to, or any possibility of, missing or mourning a lost object when absence can be undone through omnipotent thinking and denial.

The nature of the transference in a depressive mode has its own distinct qualities. In a paranoid-schizoid mode, transference is based upon the wish and the belief that one has emotionally recreated an earlier object relationship in the present relationship; in a depressive mode, transference represents an unconscious attempt to recapture something of one's experience with an earlier object in the present relationship. This latter form of transference is rooted in the context of the sadness of knowing that the relationship with the original object is a part of the past that one will never have again. At the same time, the past is never lost completely in a depressive mode in that one can repeat something of the experience with the original object in a relationship with the new object (Ogden, 1986). This, for example, under normal circumstances, makes the waning of the Oedipus complex possible. The little girl, for example, experiences sadness in her eventual acceptance of the fact that she will not be able to have the unconsciously wished-for romantic and sexual relationship with her father. The pain of this renunciation is bearable in part because the experience with the father is kept alive transferentially in relationships with new objects, and will form an important core of her mature, adult love relationships (cf. Loewald, 1979; see also Chapter 5).

The depressive mode of generating experience that has been schematically described constitutes a dialectical pole that exists only in relation to the paranoid-schizoid and autistic-contiguous poles. In the never-attained ideal of the depressive mode, analytic discourse occurs between interpreting subjects, each attempting to use words to mediate between himself and his experience of the other.

This discourse between subjects is frequently blocked by unconscious thoughts and feelings that the subject finds too frightening or unacceptable to put into words. I am referring here not only to frightening and unacceptable sexual and aggressive wishes, but also to other sorts of fears such as the unconscious anxiety that aspects of oneself are so private and so central to an endangered sense of being alive that the very act of communication will endanger the integrity of the self. Still another form of anxiety that disrupts the intersubjective discourse is the fear that one's life-sustaining ties to one's internal objects may be jeopardized through any sort of discourse in which one relinquishes control over one's internal object world by sharing knowledge of it with another (Ogden, 1983).

The analyst and analysand attempt to understand the "leading edge of anxiety" that constitutes the principal source of the disruption of the intersubjective discourse at a given moment. In a depressive mode, that anxiety is always object-related in that the unconscious reasons for feeling fearful, guilty, ashamed and the like have to do with overdetermined unconscious phantasies[3] involving internal and external objects. The derivatives of these unconscious object-related phantasies constitute the content of the analytic transference–countertransference experience.

The analyst has no means of understanding the patient except through his or her own emotionally colored perceptions of and responses to the patient. Of these perceptions and responses, only a small proportion are conscious, and it is therefore imperative that the analyst learn to detect, read, and make use of his own shifting unconscious state as it unfolds in the analytic discourse. For example, early in his analysis a patient, Mr. M., was talking with apparently great intensity of feeling about his affection for and loyalty to his wife, and the fulfillment he found in their sexual relationship. I had no conscious reason for doubting his sincerity. However, I

---

[3]Fantasying is a mental activity with conscious and dynamically unconscious dimensions. In this volume I use the term *phantasy*, spelled with a *ph*, to denote the unconscious dimensions of this mental activity. *Fantasy*, spelled with an *f*, is used to refer to the more conscious facets of this psychic activity, for example, daydreams, conscious childhood sexual theories, and conscious masturbatory narratives (cf. Isaacs, 1952).

noted a passing thought of my own that was as ephemeral as a dream as it recedes while one is awakening. I made a conscious attempt to struggle against the weight of repression in an effort to recapture it. The thought that I was repressing was infused with a somewhat smug pleasure in the self-protective privacy inherent in the role of analyst vis-à-vis the analysand. I was feeling safe in this peculiar relationship in which only the patient's "dirty laundry" is "aired." My thoughts then went to the question of what dirty laundry I suspected I was pretending to be free of at that moment.

These questions helped alert me to the possibility that the patient was at the time disavowing his anxiety in relation to the ideas he was discussing. As Mr. M.'s associations continued, his fears concerning his wife's genitals were very subtly hinted at as he discussed the sexual intercourse they had had the previous night. He said that he very much enjoyed their lovemaking in "complete darkness" and mentioned in passing that he had washed his penis afterward.

This use of the intersubjective resonance of unconscious processes occurring in individuals experiencing one another as subjects is paradigmatic of the unconscious-preconscious level of empathy in a depressive mode. This process can be thought of as involving the analyst's unconscious projection of himself into the patient's unconscious experience of himself and his internal objects; the analyst's unconscious identification with the patient's unconscious experience of himself and his internal objects; and the creation of an unconscious intersubjective third ("the Other" [Lacan, 1953]) between the patient and analyst. However it is described, it is a process in which the analyst makes available to the patient his own unconscious chain of symbolic meanings through which he

attempts to experience something similar to the unconscious experience of the patient, but in a less intense way
and in a less conflicted and less powerfully repressed or
split-off way.

Having described a conception of the depressive
mode of experience, it is necessary to reiterate that no
such entity exists; every facet of human experience is the
outcome of a dialectic constituted by the interplay of
depressive, paranoid-schizoid, and autistic-contiguous
modes. As will be discussed later, even symptomatology
generated in response to a conflict of subjective desire
(for example, conflicted Oedipal desires, fears, and
loyalties) is only partially constructed in a depressive
mode. At this point, I will delineate features of each of
the other two poles of the dialectic of experience. Again,
for purposes of clarity, this will be done as if each mode
could be isolated from the other and viewed in its purest
form.

Experience in a Paranoid-Schizoid Mode

The *paranoid-schizoid* position is Melanie Klein's (1946,
1952a, 1957, 1958) conception of a psychological organization more primitive than the depressive position. Klein
(1948) conceived of the paranoid-schizoid position as
having its origins in the first quarter of the first year of
life. Again, the emphasis in this chapter will be shifted
from Klein's diachronic conception of a sequence of
structures or developmental phases, to a consideration of
the dialectical interplay of synchronic modes.

The paranoid-schizoid mode of generating experience is based heavily upon splitting as a defense and as a
way of organizing experience. Whereas the depressive

mode operates predominantly in the service of containment of experience, including psychological pain, the
paranoid-schizoid mode is more evenly divided between
efforts at managing psychic pain and efforts at the
evacuation of pain through the defensive use of omnipotent thinking, denial, and the creation of discontinuities
of experience.

In a paranoid-schizoid mode, the experience of
loving and hating the same object generates intolerable
anxiety, which constitutes the principal psychological
dilemma to be managed. This problem is handled in large
part by separating loving and hating facets of oneself
from loving and hating facets of the object. Only in this
way can the individual safely love the object, in a state of
uncontaminated security, and safely hate without the fear
of damaging the loved object.

Splitting defensively renders object-related experience of a given emotional valence (for example, the
relationship of a loving self to a loving object) discontin-
uous from object-related experience of other valences (for
example, the relationship of a hating self to a hating
object). Each time a good object is disappointing, it is no
longer experienced as a good object—nor even as a
disappointing good object—but as the discovery of a bad
object in what had been masquerading as a good one.
Instead of the experience of ambivalence, there is the
experience of unmasking the truth. This results in a
continual rewriting of history such that the present
experience of the object is projected backward and
forward in time creating an eternal present that has only
a superficial resemblance to time as experienced in a
depressive mode.

The defensive use of discontinuity of experience
(splitting) is commonly encountered in work with patients

suffering from borderline and schizophrenic disorders.
When the patient is disappointed, hurt, angry, jealous,
and so on, he feels that he sees with powerful clarity that
he has been duped by the analyst and that he is finally
perceiving the reality of the situation as it is and as it
always has been: "The fact of the matter is that I've
deluded myself about you for a long time. It is obvious to
me now that you have absolutely no regard for me,
otherwise you wouldn't forget fundamental things about
me like my girlfriend's name that I've mentioned a
thousand times."

Rewriting of history leads to a brittleness and insta-
bility of object relations that are in continual states of
reversal. There is no stable, shared experience of the
history of the patient–analyst relationship that can form a
framework and container for present experience. In this
mode of experience there is an almost continuous background of anxiety deriving from the fact that the individual unconsciously feels as if he or she is perpetually in
uncharted territory in the presence of unpredictable
strangers. Analytic theory need not appeal to the concept
of the death instinct to account for the anxiety occurring
within such a brittle container for psychological experience.

In a paranoid-schizoid mode, there is virtually no
space between symbol and symbolized; the two are
emotionally equivalent. This mode of symbolization,
termed *symbolic equation* (Segal, 1957), generates a two-
dimensional form of experience in which everything is
what it is. There is almost no interpreting subject mediating between the percept (whether external or internal)
and one's thoughts and feelings about that which one is
perceiving. The patient operating in a predominantly
paranoid-schizoid mode may say, "You can't tell me I

don't see what I see." In this mode, thoughts and feelings are not experienced as personal creations but as facts, things-in-themselves, that simply exist. Perception and interpretation are experienced as one and the same. The patient is trapped in the manifest since surface and depth are indistinguishable. That which would be viewed as interpretation from the perspective of the depressive mode, would be experienced in a paranoid-schizoid mode as an attempt to "twist the facts," to distract, deceive, and confuse through the "use of psychological bullshit."

Transference in a paranoid-schizoid mode has been termed *"delusional"* (Little, 1958) or *"psychotic"* (Searles, 1963) transference. The analyst is not experienced as *similar to* the original childhood object, he *is* the original object. For example, a therapist made some inquiries during a therapy hour about the details of a physical complaint that his patient, A., was discussing. The patient experienced this as an anxious, intrusive overreaction on the part of the therapist that led the patient to experience the therapist as having *become* her mother (not simply as being like her mother). The following day the patient consulted her internist who later in bewilderment called the therapist and said that A. had introduced herself by saying, "I'm A.'s mother. I'm very worried about A.'s illness and would like to ask you some questions about it." In this way, the patient became her therapist-mother and enacted the overanxiousness and intrusiveness of the therapist-mother.

In the absence of the capacity to mediate between oneself and one's experience, a very limited form of subjectivity is generated. In a paranoid-schizoid mode, the self is predominantly a self as object, a self that is buffeted by thoughts, feelings, and perceptions as if they were external forces or physical objects occupying or bombarding oneself. An adolescent schizophrenic patient would violently turn his head in order to "shake" (get rid of) a thought that was tormenting him. Another schizophrenic patient requested an X-ray film in order to be able to see what it was inside of him that was driving him crazy. Still another patient "took a big shit" in the therapist's waiting room toilet before each session in order not to harm the therapist with his toxic inner contents during the session.

When working with patients generating experience in a predominantly paranoid-schizoid mode, one must couch one's interventions in language that reflects the concreteness of the patient's experience; otherwise, patient and analyst have the experience of talking in a way that, in the words of one such patient, "completely misses one another." One does not talk about the patient's feeling that he is like a robot, one talks with the patient about what it feels like to be a robot; one does not talk with the patient about his feeling that he is infatuated with a woman, one talks with him about what he feels when he believes he is possessed or haunted by a woman; one does not talk about the patient's wish to be understood by the therapist, one talks about the patient's conviction that the therapist — if he is to be of any value at all to the patient — must think the patient's thoughts and feel the patient's feelings.

Psychological defense in a paranoid-schizoid mode is based in large part on the principle that one secures safety by separating the endangered from the endangering (cf. Grotstein, 1985). This is the psychological meaning of splitting. All defenses in a paranoid-schizoid mode are derived from this principle; for example, projection is an effort to place an endangering (or endangered) aspect of self or object outside of the self while retaining the endangered (or endangering) aspect of self or object within. The other defenses in this mode of generating experience — introjection, projective identification, denial, and idealization — can be seen as variations on this theme.

The paranoid-schizoid mode is characterized by omnipotent thinking through which the emotional complexities of loving and hating are magically "resolved," or — more accurately — precluded from psychic reality. In this mode, guilt (as it exists in a depressive mode), simply does not arise; it has no place in the emotional vocabulary of this more primitive mode. Since one's objects, like oneself, are perceived in this mode as objects rather than as subjects, one cannot care about them or have concern for them.[4] There is little to empathize with since one's objects are not experienced as people with thoughts and feelings, but rather as loved, hated, or feared forces or things that impinge on oneself. Other people can be valued for what they can do for one, but one does not have *concern* for them — as one does not have concern for one's possessions, even the most important of them. As described earlier, an object can be damaged or used up, but only a subject can be hurt or injured.

In a paranoid-schizoid mode, what might become a feeling of guilt, is dissipated through, for example, the use of omnipotent reparative phantasies. The injury to the object is denied through the use of a magical remedy

---

[4]Because the paranoid-schizoid mode never exists in isolation from the depressive mode (and the autistic-contiguous mode), the concept of the self-as-object (completely dissociated from the experience of self as subject) is phenomenologically meaningless. Due to the dialectical structure of experience, self-experience is never completely devoid of a sense of "I-ness," and one's objects are never simply objects altogether devoid of subjectivity.

that is intended to expunge from history the harm that one has done. History is rewritten and the need for guilt is thereby obviated. For instance, a patient operating heavily in a paranoid-schizoid mode often would laugh and say that he was only kidding after having said something extremely cruel to his wife. Having said, "You know I was only kidding," he felt that he had undone the damage by magically changing the assault into something humorous (by re-naming it). When his wife refused to participate in this magical rewriting of history, the patient would escalate his efforts at joviality and begin to treat her with contempt, accusing her of being a baby for not being able to "take it."

This attempt to make use of paranoid-schizoid defenses (magical reparation, denial, and rewriting of history) for the purpose of warding off depressive anxiety (guilt and the fear of the loss of the object due to one's destructiveness) constitutes a manic defense. Loewald (1979) has described the way in which self-punishment can be similarly used to dissipate feelings that threaten to become an experience of guilt. In this case, one uses an omnipotent phantasy that the self-punishment eradicates the present and past existence of the crime and therefore there is no reason to feel guilty.

Similarly, in a paranoid-schizoid mode one does not miss a lost or absent object; one denies the loss, short-circuits the feeling of sadness, and replaces the object (person) with another person or with oneself. Since the new person or aspect of self is emotionally equivalent to the lost object, nothing has changed; there is no need to mourn what is still present (cf. Searles, 1982). For example, a patient explained that my vacation turned out to be a "blessing in disguise" since he had learned through it that he was not nearly so dependent on me as I had led him to believe. In this case, an aspect of self was used to magically replace the absent object. In my work with this patient, each of my absences was regularly followed by an enactment of manic defenses of various forms, such as threatened disruptions of treatment (which he "no longer needed") or grudging agreement to continue analysis "if that's what you think is best."

Object relatedness in a paranoid-schizoid mode is predominantly in the form of projective identification (Grotstein, 1981; Klein, 1946; Ogden, 1979, 1982b). This psychological-interpersonal process reflects many of the other facets of the paranoid-schizoid mode discussed thus far. It is based on the omnipotent phantasy that an aspect of self (which is either endangered or endangering) can be placed in another person in such a way that "the recipient" is controlled from within (Klein, 1955). In this way, one safeguards an endangered aspect of self, and at the same time attempts to omnipotently control an object relationship by treating the object as an incompletely separate container for aspects of oneself. This facet of the process of projective identification involves an evacuative method of managing psychological strain.

In projective identification, the projector—by means of actual interpersonal interactions with the "recipient"—unconsciously induces feeling states in the recipient that are congruent with the "ejected" feelings. In addition to serving defensive purposes, this constitutes a fundamental form of communication and object relatedness. The recipient of the projective identification can sometimes retrospectively become aware that he is "playing a part . . . in somebody else's phantasy" (Bion, 1959a, p. 149). Projective identification is a "direct communication" (Winnicott, 1971c, p. 54) in that it is unmediated by interpreting subjects; instead, it is predominantly a communication between the unconscious of one person and that of another. For this reason, it is often experienced by the recipient as coercive. There is no choice: one not only finds oneself playing a role in someone else's internal drama, one feels unable to stop doing so. The recipient feels controlled from within. If he is able to contain the induced feelings without simply dumping them back into the projector, a shift in the relationship between the projector and the recipient can occur that leads to psychological growth. The "processing" of a projective identification by the recipient is not simply a matter of returning modified psychological contents to the projector. Rather, it is a matter of altering the intersubjective mode of containment generated by the interacting pair, thus generating a new way of experiencing the old psychological contents. It is not so much that psychological contents are modified; it is the intersubjective context of those contents that is modified.

This conception of psychological change is not limited to the understanding of projective identification. Rather, what we have arrived at in the course of this discussion is a basic principle of all psychological growth including that which occurs in the analytic process. Psychological growth occurs not simply as a result of the modification of unconscious psychological contents; in addition, what changes is the experiential context (the nature of the containment of the psychological contents). Unconscious phantasy is timeless and is never destroyed (Freud, 1911a). It is therefore misleading to talk about the eradication of an unconscious phantasy since that implies that the old phantasy is destroyed or replaced by a new one. It is not the unconscious phantasy that is destroyed or replaced; rather, the phantasy is experienced differently due to a shift in the psychological matrix within which it exists.

The idea that it is not only content but context that shifts in psychological growth was elegantly articulated by a schizophrenic patient when asked if he still had his hallucinatory voices. He replied, "Oh yes, they're still there, they just don't talk anymore." Similarly, in the course of analysis, one does not destroy the thoughts and feelings constituting the Oedipus complex (Loewald, 1979); instead one experiences the component object-related feelings differently. A patient, Mr. K., said in small bits over the course of his fourth year of analysis, "I am still aware that when I am with women teachers I could become extremely anxious if I were to allow myself to experience them (as I used to) as mothers whom I am afraid of having sexual feelings and fantasies about. But I do have some choice in the matter now and I realize that there was some pleasure and excitement in imagining that I could be sufficiently special (more special than my father and brothers) to get my mother to stop being a mother and start being a wife to me." What had been achieved by this patient was not simply a change in the content of his unconscious phantasy. The Oedipus complex had not been "destroyed" or "overcome." Rather, the psychological context for the experiencing of his Oedipal wishes and fears had undergone change. Previously, the set of unconscious Oedipal desires and prohibitions had been characterized by powerful concreteness and immediacy. Mr. K. initially said that he had no idea why he had anxiety "attacks" when talking with women teachers. "It is something that just happens to me and there is no reason for it. I know there is no real danger. The anxiety just goes through me like electricity." As a result, the patient had developed compulsive study habits in an effort to become a perfect student, and he became terribly anxious before exams even though he had prepared in a way that he recognized to be "overkill."

Oedipal feelings and phantasies are always generated in part in a depressive mode. The Oedipal dilemma would have no power or poignancy if it were not the problem of a subject (for example, the boy) who hates — and thus wishes to be forever rid of — the same father he loves. In other words, it is a dilemma rooted in subjectivity, whole object relations, ambivalence, and historicity. However, important facets of this unconscious conflict and its resultant symptomatology (anxiety attacks for example) are experienced largely in a paranoid-schizoid mode. For example, Mr. K. initially experienced his anxiety attacks not as a form of, or reaction to, his feelings and fearful thoughts, but as a force sweeping over him that frightened him. The patient's female teachers were unconsciously experienced as not simply like his mother, but *the same as* his mother; otherwise the full power of the incestuous danger would not have presented itself in such a concrete way. (Dream material in this phase of analysis included the frightening shifting back and forth of the identity of older women figures, which resulted in a feeling on the part of Mr. K. that he "didn't know who was who.") The patient was clearly not psychotic; but the transference to his female teachers was simultaneously experienced in both paranoid–schizoid and depressive modes with a tendency for the dialectical interplay between the two to "collapse" in the direction of the paranoid-schizoid mode during anxiety attacks (Ogden, 1985b). In his attacks of anxiety, there was very little of a subject mediating between the patient and the terrifying thing happening to him.

From this point of view, psychoanalysis is a method of treatment designed not only to help the patient modify unconscious phantasy content, but also, a process aimed at helping the patient to experience unconscious content differently. That is, psychoanalysis is a process directed at helping the patient shift the balance of the dialectical interplay between different modes of generating experience in relation to specific unconscious contents. What must happen in analysis is not a simple translation of psychological contents from one mode to another. The therapeutic process as I understand it involves the establishment, reestablishment, or expansion of a dialectical relationship between different modes of experience.

Before closing this section, I would like to briefly comment on the tendency among analytic thinkers, including Klein herself, to valorize the depressive mode and villainize the paranoid-schizoid mode. As Eigen (1985) has pointed out, the depressive mode is too often viewed as the full realization of the human potential. In the depressive mode, it is held that the individual develops the capacity for abstract symbolization, subjectivity and self-reflection, concern for others, guilt, and reparative wishes, all of which lead to cultural production. On the other hand, the paranoid-schizoid mode is understood as generating a psychological state in which the individual relies on splitting and projective identification for the purpose of evacuating feelings and denying reality. However, such a depiction of these modes is based on a diachronic conception of the relationship between the two, and fails to appreciate the fundamental dialectical nature of their relationship. The paranoid-schizoid mode and the depressive mode serve as essential negating and preserving contexts for one another. The depressive mode is one of integration, resolution, and containment, and if unopposed, leads to certainty, stagnation, closure, arrogance, and deadness (Bion, 1962, 1963; Eigen, 1985). The paranoid-schizoid mode provides the necessary splitting of linkages and opening up of the closures of the depressive position, thus reestablishing the possibility of fresh linkages and fresh thoughts. The integrative thrust of the depressive mode in turn provides the necessary antithesis for the paranoid-schizoid mode in limiting the chaos generated by the fragmentation of thought, the discontinuity of experience, and the splitting of self and object.

The Autistic-Contiguous Mode of Generating Experience

The conceptions of the paranoid-schizoid and depressive modes discussed thus far represent ideas derived predominantly from the work of Klein and Bion. The conception of a dialectic of experience constituted exclusively by these two modes is incomplete, insofar as it fails to recognize an even more primitive presymbolic, sensory-dominated mode that I will refer to as the *autistic-contiguous mode*. The conception of an autistic-contiguous pole of the dialectic of experience represents an integration, interpretation, and extension of aspects of the work of Bick (1968, 1986); Meltzer (Meltzer 1975, 1986; Meltzer et al., 1975); and Tustin (1972, 1980, 1981, 1984, 1986). Each of these authors was strongly influenced by Bion's (1962, 1963) conception of the container and the contained, as well as by his theory of thinking. In this chapter, space allows for only a brief introduction to a discussion of this mode of experience. (In Chapter 3, the concept of an autistic-contiguous position will be discussed in detail.)

The autistic-contiguous position is a primitive psychological organization operative from birth that generates the most elemental forms of human experience.[5] It is a sensory-dominated mode in which the most inchoate sense of self is built upon the rhythm of sensation (Tustin, 1984), particularly the sensations at the skin surface (Bick, 1968). The autistic-contiguous mode[6] of

---

[5]The autistic-contiguous position is conceptualized in this book not as a prepsychological (biological) phase of development in which the infant lives in a world cut off from dynamic relations with external objects; rather, it is conceived of as a psychological organization in which sensory modes of generating experience are organized into defensive processes in the face of perceived danger. Under circumstances of extreme, protracted anxiety, these defenses become hypertrophied and rigidified and come to constitute a pathologically autistic psychological structure. The development of a normal autistic-contiguous organization can occur only within the unfolding relationship with the mother as environment and the mother as object (cf. Winnicott, 1963a).

[6]I have termed the most primitive of the modes of experience *the autistic-contiguous mode* in order to roughly parallel the method of naming the paranoid-schizoid mode, which takes its name from both the form of psychological organization and the form of defense associated with it. In the autistic-contiguous mode, psychic organization is derived in large part from sensory contiguity, that is, connections are established through the experience of sensory surfaces "touching" one another. Breakdown of this organization leads to the implementation of autistic defenses that are described in this book.

It must be borne in mind throughout the book that the term *autistic* is being used to refer to specific features of a universal sensory-dominated mode of experience, and not to a form of severe childhood psychopathology. It would be as absurd to view infants or adults as being pathologically autistic while relying heavily on an

experiencing is a presymbolic, sensory mode and is therefore extremely difficult to capture in words. Rhythmicity and experiences of sensory contiguity contribute to the earliest psychological organization in this mode. Both rhythmicity and experiences of surface contiguity are fundamental to a person's earliest relations with objects: the nursing experience and the experience of being held, rocked, spoken to and sung to in his mother's arms. These experiences are "object-related" in a very specific and very limited sense of the word. The relationship to the object in this mode is certainly not a relationship between subjects, as in a depressive mode; nor is it a relationship between objects, as in a paranoid-schizoid mode. Rather, it is a relationship of shape to the feeling of enclosure, of beat to the feeling of rhythm, of hardness to the feeling of edgedness. Sequences, symmetries, periodicity, skin-to-skin "molding" are all examples of contiguities that are the ingredients out of which the beginnings of rudimentary self-experience arise. The experience of "self" at this point is simply that of a nonreflective state of sensory "going on being" (Winnicott, 1956, p. 303) derived from "body needs" which only "gradually become ego needs as a psychology gradually emerges out of the [mother–infant's] imaginative elaboration of physical experience" (p. 304).[7]

---

autistic-contiguous mode of generating experience, as it would be to think of them as being paranoid-schizophrenics while organizing experience in a paranoid-schizoid mode, or as being depressed while operating in a predominantly depressive mode.

[7]Stern (1985), from a psychoanalytic developmental-observational vantage point, states, "Infants [from birth] . . . take sensations, perceptions, actions, cognitions, internal states of motivation and states of (non-self-reflective) consciousness and experience them directly in terms of intensities, shapes, temporal patterns, vitality

Early experiences of sensory contiguity define a surface (the beginnings of what will become a sense of place) on which experience is created and organized. These sensory experiences with "objects" (which only an outside observer would be aware of as objects) are the media through which the earliest forms of organized and organizing experience are created.

Contiguity of surfaces (e.g., "molded" skin surfaces, harmonic sounds, rhythmic rocking or sucking, symmetrical shapes) generate the experience of a sensory surface rather than the feeling of two surfaces coming together either in mutually differentiating opposition or in merger. There is practically no sense of inside and outside or self and other; rather, what is important is the pattern, boundedness, shape, rhythm, texture, hardness, softness, warmth, coldness, and so on.

A 29-year-old patient, Mrs. L., came to an analytic hour after having just spent time with her mother, and felt, for reasons that she "could not put her finger on," as if she were in a state of such severe anxiety and diffuse tension that the only way to end the state of tension would be to cut herself with a razor all over her body. It had taken great effort on her part to come to the session instead of cutting herself as she had done in the past. The patient cried uncontrollably during the hour. I interpreted as much of the situation as I thought I understood on the basis of what I knew about the patient's relationship to her mother and the connection between these feelings and the transference–coun-

---

affects, categorical affects, and hedonic tones" (p. 67). This earliest mode of experience operates throughout life "out of awareness as the experiential matrix" (p. 67) for all succeeding subjective states.

tertransference anxieties of the previous few sessions. Mrs. L. said that she felt as if she were "coming apart at the seams." I said that I thought she was feeling as if she were coming apart in the most literal way, and that she felt as if her skin were already lacerated in the way she had imagined lacerating herself.

It was late in the afternoon and getting cold in the office. I said, "It's cold in here," and got up to turn on the heater. She said, "It is," and seemed to calm down soon after that. She said that for reasons that she did not understand she had been extremely "touched" by my saying that it was cold and by turning the heater on: "It was such an ordinary thing to say and do." I believe that my putting the heater on acknowledged a shared experience of the growing coldness in the air and contributed to the creation of a sensory surface between us. I was using my own feelings and sensations in a largely unconscious "ordinary way" (perhaps like "an ordinary devoted mother" [Winnicott, 1949]) which felt to the patient as if I had physically touched her and held her together. The sensory surface mutually created in that way was the opposite of the experience of "coming apart at the seams"; it facilitated a mending of her psychological-sensory surface which felt as if it had been shredded in the course of the patient's interaction with her mother.

This sensory "holding" (Winnicott, 1960a) dimension of the analytic relationship and setting operated in conjunction with the binding power of symbolic interpretation (formulated on the basis of the intersubjectivity of the transference–countertransference).

Clearly, the experience just presented was not an example of "pure and undiluted" experience in an autistic-contiguous mode. As is always the case, the autistic-contiguous mode "borrows from" (interpenetrates with) the paranoid-schizoid mode in the creation of phantasy representations for sensory-dominated experience, as well as borrowing upon features of a depressive mode including elements of subjectivity, historicity, and symbolization proper.

There is a crucial distinction between a purely physiological reflex arc and experience in an autistic-contiguous mode despite the fact that both can be described in nonsymbolic, bodily terms. Although the physiological reflex has a locus (from an outside observer's point of view), a locus is different from the beginnings of a sense of a place in which experience is occurring; the physiological reflex may to an observer have periodicity, but periodicity is different from the feeling of rhythm; the physiological reflex may have a temporal and spatial beginning and end, but that is not the same as a feeling of boundedness. The rudiments of the sensory experience of self in an autistic-contiguous mode have nothing to do with the representation of one's affective states, either idiographically or fully symbolically. The sensory experience *is* the infant in this mode, and the abrupt disruption of shape, symmetry, rhythm, skin moldedness, and so on, marks the end of the infant.

Tustin (1984) attempted to communicate the nature of experience at the infant's skin surface by asking us to try to experience the chair we are sitting on not as an object, but simply as a sensory impression on our skin: "Forget your chair. Instead, feel your seat pressing against the seat of the chair. It will make a 'shape.' If you wriggle, the shape will change. Those 'shapes' will be entirely personal to you" (pp. 281–282). In the autistic-contiguous mode, there is neither a chair nor one's

buttocks, simply a sensory "impression" in the most literal
sense of the word. Tustin describes two sorts of sensory
impressions constituting normal early experience: soft
impressions which she terms *autistic shapes* (1984) and hard
angular impressions which she terms *autistic objects* (1980).
The difference between these experiences of sensory
surface constitutes forms of definition of experiental
content within this mode. Experience of an autistic shape
is the feeling of softness that much later we associate with
ideas like security, safety, relaxation, warmth, and affection. The words that seem to me to be closest to the
sensory level of the experience are the words *soothing* and
comforting. It is not a matter of mother comforting me — it
is simply a soothing sensory experience.

A relationship to an autistic shape is different from
a relationship to a transitional object (Winnicott, 1951) in
that the "otherness" of the autistic shape is of almost no
significance. In transitional phenomena, the experience
centers on the paradox that the object is at the same time
created and discovered by the subject, and that therefore
the object always has one foot in the world outside of the
individual's omnipotence. This is clearly not the case in
relationships to autistic shapes and objects.

Mr. R. began analysis and found to his great distress
that he literally could not think of anything to say. He
felt utterly blank and empty. He had looked forward to
the beginning of analysis but found the analytic experience terrifying. He had expected to be able to talk
without difficulty. Mr. R. unconsciously managed to
create a sensory base for himself by filling what he later
called the "holes" both in himself (his inability to think
or talk), and in the analytic relationship (which he
experienced as nonexistent), by focusing intently on a

rectangular shape that he discerned in the pattern of lines and texture on the ceiling above the couch. These "holes" were subsequently understood in part as derivatives of the patient's early experience of the "holes" in the early mother–infant relationship associated with his mother's profound postpartum depression for which she was briefly hospitalized. She told him during the course of the analysis that she had held him as a baby only when "absolutely necessary." He had been allowed to cry in his crib for hours on end while his mother hid in her room.

In contrast, the experience of an autistic object is the feeling of a hard, angular impression upon the skin that is experienced as if it were a hard shell-like quality of the skin. It is associated with the most diffuse sense of danger, and with what may be represented in a paranoid-schizoid mode by phantasies of a hard shell formed by the skin surface to be used as a protective armor.

Mrs. M., a 35-year old attorney, developed—during an acute regressive phase of treatment—an extreme muscular rigidity that led to cramping of her muscles, particularly in the neck. She would frequently massage her cramped muscles during the sessions. These symptoms clearly had features resembling a catatonic state wherein defense against unconscious anger is usually central. However, the current transference–countertransference experience in this case did not center around the patient's fears of her destructiveness in relation to herself or to me. Rather, the material just prior to the acute regression had been organized around feelings of utter vulnerability represented in dreams by images of being a pincushion. This was

understood as a derivative of Mrs. M.'s feeling, which
we had previously discussed, of being powerless to
resist being taken over by her mother's (and my)
projections of ourselves into her. As a result, over time
I interpreted the acute regression in Mrs. M.'s analysis
as an effort by her to create a hardness in her body that
would serve as a way of resisting my attempts to get
inside of her in order — as she perceived it — to control
her and turn her into what I needed her to be for me.
Mrs. M.'s massaging of her muscles was viewed both
as a way of creating a sensory surface on which to
locate herself, and as a way of reassuring herself that
the surface was a hard protective one. (During this
same regressed phase of analysis, the patient presented
no phantasies or dreams of being invaded or of having
a shell; experience was predominantly in a sensory
mode.) The tension diminished as the sensory experience was reconnected with words by means of verbal
interpretation.

I conduct all phases of analysis and psychoanalytic
therapy (despite major shifts in the dialectical balance of
the three modes of experience) on the basis of the
principle that there is always a facet of the personality, no
matter how hidden or disguised, operating in a depressive
mode and therefore capable of utilizing verbally symbolized interpretations (Bion, 1957; Boyer and Giovacchini,
1967). Often the succession of the patient's associations,
in conjunction with affective shifts in a given meeting or
series of meetings, serve as evidence that the patient has
heard and made use of the analyst's interpretation.
Sometimes one must wait for years before the patient
gives direct evidence (e.g., by reminding the analyst of an
interpretation made at a time when the patient seemed

incapable of operating in a depressive mode) that he or she has utilized the interpretation.[8]

The breakdown of the continuity of sensory-dominated experience being described results in the anxiety that Bick (1968) and Meltzer (Meltzer et al., 1975), on the basis of their work with pathologically autistic children as well as with healthier children and adults, describe as the experience of one's skin becoming a sieve through which one's insides leak out and fall into endless, shapeless space devoid of surface or definition of any sort (see also Rosenfeld, 1984). Bion (1959b) refers to experience stripped of containment and meaning as "nameless dread." (Perhaps the term *formless dread* might better reflect the nature of anxiety in the autistic-contiguous mode since the experience of shapes, rhythms, and patterns are the only "names" that exist in this mode.)

Mrs. N., a 52-year-old woman with an extremely unstable sense of continuity of being, spent long periods of time in every therapy hour silently attempting to picture phone numbers, birth dates, street numbers, and so on of all of the people that she had known since childhood. In the middle of one of these extended ruminative silences, the phone in my office rang and was promptly answered by my answering machine. Mrs. N. was clearly shaken by this and left the office. This was the first time during the course of

---

[8] I believe that while there is always an aspect of the patient functioning in a depressive mode (a "non-psychotic part of the personality" [Bion, 1957]), there are always at the same time other aspects of experience that are defensively foreclosed from the realm of the psychological, for example, by means of the creation of psychosomatic illness (McDougall, 1974), alexithymia (Nemiah, 1977), and forms of "non-experience" (Ogden, 1980).

her treatment that she had done so. She returned in about five minutes. Much later in the therapy, Mrs. N. told me, with a mixture of shame and relief, that she had left the room on that occasion to go to the bathroom because of her feeling that she had soiled herself with feces or urine. This experience was not represented at the time in the form of thoughts and was primarily a physical sensation. Only in retrospect could the patient describe it as a feeling of having been "cut into" by the unexpected disruption of her ruminative thoughts. Mrs. N. had a long history, beginning in early childhood, of violent disruptions of her self-experience. For example, the patient reported that her mother would tie her arms and legs to her bedposts at night, when she was 6 years old, in order to prevent her from masturbating.

The terror ensuing from such disruption of the continuity of sensory experience calls into play forms of defense specific to this mode of experience. Bick (1968, 1986) describes a type of defense that she refers to as "second skin formation." This is a self-protective effort at resurrecting a feeling of the continuity and integrity of one's surface.[9] An example of pathological second skin

---

[9]Meltzer (Meltzer et al., 1975), building upon the work of Bick (1968), introduced the term *adhesive identification* to describe a form of identification more primitive than either introjective or projective identification. In an autistic-contiguous mode (which Meltzer refers to as the "world of two-dimensionality" [p. 225]), one utilizes adhesive identification in an attempt to create or defensively reconstitute a rudimentary sense of the cohesiveness of one's surface. The surface of the other is utilized as a substitute for an incompletely developed or deteriorating sense of one's own surface. Examples of the means by which the surface of the object is defensively "adhered

formation is the development of infantile eczema that Spitz (1965) understood as a psychosomatic disorder resulting from insufficiency or inadequacy of parental holding in the first weeks and months of life. The continual scratching (often leading to the necessity of wrapping the infant's hands in gauze to prevent severe skin damage and infection) is understood from this perspective as the infant's desperate attempt to restore (through heightened skin sensation) a surface by means of which the terror of leakage and of falling into shapeless space is allayed.

Wrapping a hospitalized patient snugly in sheets (while he is continually accompanied and related to by an empathic staff member) is an effective and humane way of treating someone who is experiencing the terror of impending annihilation in the form of the dispersal of the self into unbounded space. This form of intervention represents an attempt to almost literally supply the patient with a second skin by means of the provision of a firm, palpable, containing sensory and interpersonal surface.

Common forms of second skin formation encountered clinically with adult patients in psychotherapy and analysis include unremitting eye contact that begins in the waiting room and is only painfully terminated by the

---

to" in adhesive identification include imitation, mimicry, and clinging forms of sensory connectedness to an object that "can hold [one's] attention and thereby be experienced, momentarily at least, as holding the parts of the [sensory-dominated] personality together" (Bick, 1968, p. 49).

Tustin (1986) prefers the term *adhesive equation* to the term *adhesive identification* since, in this defensive process, the individual's body is equated with the object in the most concrete, sensory way.

closing of the consulting room door at the end of the hour; constant chatter on the part of the patient filling every moment of the session leaving hardly a moment of silence; continual holding of one object or another that is either brought to the session or picked up from the analyst's office (e.g., a tissue); perpetual humming or repeating of sentences or phrases, particularly when a silence might otherwise ensue.

Tustin (1980, 1981, 1984, 1986) has explored the defensive use of autistic objects and shapes in the face of threatened disruption of the sensory continuity of self. Autistic shapes and objects offer a form of self-soothing that is "perfect" in a way that no human being can possibly be. The self-soothing activity, whether it be hair twirling, stroking the lobe of the ear, thumb sucking, sucking on the inner surface of the check, rocking, tapping one's foot, humming, imagining symmetrical geometric designs or series of numbers, is absolutely and reliably present. Such activities always have precisely the same sensory qualities and rhythms; they never evidence shifts in mood, and are never a fraction of a second late when they are needed. No human being can provide such machinelike reliability. The individual has absolute control over the autistic activity; however, at the same time, the autistic activity can tyrannize the individual (Tustin, 1984). The tyrannical power of the activity derives from the fact that an individual relying on an autistic mode of defense is absolutely dependent on the ability of the perfect recreation of the sensory[10] experience to protect

---

[10]Boyer's (1986) version of the "fundamental rule" incorporates a full appreciation of the sensory dimension of the analytic experience. He at times directly and at times indirectly (e.g., through the questions he poses) asks his patients to attempt to notice and put into words the

him against unbearable terror ("formless dread"). I have
been impressed by the way in which both aspects of this
tyranny — the individual's control of the autistic activity,
and the activity's control over him — play important roles
even in the psychoanalysis of adult patients who have
achieved the capacity for stably generating experience in
a predominantly depressive mode.

A 42-year-old patient, Dr. E., a psychotherapist, became enraged if I was a minute late in beginning his
analytic hour. (He wore a digital watch.) Dr. E. said
that he knew I understood the importance of "the
frame," and that if I violated it in this egregious way,
I must not care about him or the analysis in the least.
The "frame" was not just an idea for this patient, but a
palpable feeling as tangible, hard, and enclosing as the
metal frame around a picture. This man had indeed
become addicted to the analytic frame as an autistic
object. Dr. E. made it clear that he needed not simply
reliability in our "relationship," but absolute certainty.
As a result, he attempted to control everything including my thoughts and feelings. He would continually tell me what I was thinking and feeling; in that way
he could attempt to ensure that he would never be
surprised or disappointed by me. Interpretations of
mine that incorporated an idea or perspective that Dr.
E. had not yet thought of were extremely distressing to
him because they reflected the fact that I had thoughts
that he had not created and therefore did not control in
an absolute way. This set of feelings and this form of

---

thoughts, feelings, and *physical sensations* that they experience in the
sessions. He also asks the same of himself in his efforts to utilize his
countertransference experience (Boyer, 1983, 1987).

relatedness are usually understood in terms of anal-erotic obsession, omnipotence, and projective identification. These are no doubt accurate descriptions of this symptomatology and form of relatedness, but they need to be supplemented by an understanding of the way in which the experience also involves tyrannizing relatedness to an autistic object.

The topic of countertransference responses to analytic experience in an autistic-contiguous mode can only briefly be touched upon here. The analyst's feelings often include feelings of being tyrannized by an automaton (as in the case of Dr. E.), feelings of inadequacy for having no compassion with the patient or for being unable to make any connection whatever with him or her, and intense feelings of protectiveness for the patient. This relatively familiar range of feelings is not unlike the group of responses one has to patients operating in predominantly paranoid-schizoid and depressive modes. More specific to the autistic-contiguous mode of experience is countertransference experience in which bodily sensations dominate. Somatic experiences like twitching of one's hand and arm, stomach pain, feelings of bloatedness and so on are not uncommon. Very frequently the countertransference experience is associated with skin sensations such as feelings of warmth and coldness (see earlier discussion of Mrs. L. in this chapter) as well as tingling, numbness, and an exaggerated sensitivity to skin impressions like the tightness of one's tie or one's shoes. At times, the space between the patient and myself has felt as if it were filled with a warm soothing substance. Frequently, this is associated with a drowsy countertransference state that has nothing to do with boredom. It is a rather pleasant feeling of being suspended between sleep and wakefulness. (Perhaps this is the sensory dimension of Bion's [1962] idea of "reverie," a concept referring to the analyst's state of receptivity to the patient's unconscious experience and the mother's receptivity to her infant's symbolic and asymbolic [or presymbolic] experience.)

From the perspective developed in this chapter, the autistic-contiguous mode, under normal circumstances, can be seen to provide the bounded sensory "floor" (Grotstein, 1987) of experience. It offers sensory enclosure that exists in dialectical tension with the fragmenting potential of the paranoid-schizoid mode. The danger of psychosis posed by the fragmenting and evacuative processes of the paranoid-schizoid mode are contained in two ways: (1) "From above" by the binding capacity of symbolic linkages, historicity, and subjectivity of the depressive mode; and (2) "from below" by the sensory continuity, rhythmicity, and boundedness of the autistic-contiguous mode.

Summary

In this chapter, human experience is conceived of as the outcome of a dialectical relationship between three modes of experience. The autistic-contiguous mode provides a good measure of the sensory continuity and integrity of experience (the sensory "floor"); the paranoid-schizoid mode is a principal source of the immediacy of concretely symbolized experience; and the depressive mode is a principal medium through which historical subjectivity and the richness of symbolically mediated human experience is generated. Experience is always generated between the poles represented by the ideal of the pure form of each of these modes.

These modes of generating experience are analogous to empty sets each filled in their relationship with the others. Psychopathology can be thought of as forms of collapse of the richness of experience generated between these poles. Collapse may be in the direction of the autistic-contiguous pole, the paranoid-schizoid pole, or the depressive pole. Collapse toward the autistic-contiguous pole generates imprisonment in the machine-like tyranny of attempted sensory-based escape from the terror of formless dread, by means of reliance on rigid autistic defenses. Collapse into the paranoid-schizoid pole is characterized by imprisonment in a nonsubjective world of thoughts and feelings experienced in terms of frightening and protective things that simply happen, and that cannot be thought about or interpreted. Collapse in the direction of the depressive pole involves a form of isolation of oneself from one's bodily sensations, and from the immediacy of one's lived experience, leaving one devoid of spontaneity and aliveness.

3

The Autistic-Contiguous Position

The exchange of ideas constituting the British psychoanalytic discourse of the 1930s to the early 1970s revolved in large part around the work of Klein, Winnicott, Fairbairn, and Bion. Each of these analysts provided the context for—as well as a counterpoint to—the ideas generated by the others. The history of the development of British object relations theory in the last twenty years can be viewed as containing the beginnings of an exploration of an area of experience lying outside of the experiential states addressed by Klein's (1958) concepts of the paranoid-schizoid and depressive positions; by Fairbairn's (1944) conception of the internal object world; by Bion's (1962) conception of projective identification as a primitive form of defense, communication, and containment; or by Winnicott's (1971a) conception of the evolution of the mother–infant relationship and the elaboration of transitional phenomena.

The clinical and theoretical work of Esther Bick (1968, 1986), Donald Meltzer (Meltzer, 1975; Meltzer et al., 1975), and Frances Tustin (1972, 1980, 1981, 1984, 1986), developed in the context of their clinical work with autistic children, has served to define a heretofore insufficiently understood dimension of all human experience (more primitive than the paranoid-schizoid position) that I refer to as the autistic-contiguous position. The present chapter represents a synthesis, interpretation, and extension of the work of these analytic thinkers. (A partial listing of other important contributors to this area of investigation includes: J. Anthony 1958; Anzieu 1970; Bion 1962; Bower 1977; Brazelton 1981; Eimas 1975; Fordham 1977; E. Gaddini 1969, 1987; R. Gaddini 1978, 1987; Grotstein 1978, 1983; Kanner 1944; S. Klein 1980; Mahler 1952, 1968; Milner 1969 D. Rosenfeld 1984; Sander 1964; Searles 1960; Spitz 1965; Stern 1977, 1985; Trevarthan 1979; and Winnicott 1960a.)

In the previous chapter, I termed the psychological organization generating the most primitive state of being the *autistic-contiguous position.* (I used the term *position* because I view this psychological organization as a developing and ongoing mode of generating experience as opposed to a phase of development. I regard it as having equal organizing significance to the paranoid-schizoid and depressive positions and as contributing equally powerfully to the dialectic constituting human experience.) The elaboration of this primitive organization represents an integral part of normal development through which a distinctive mode of experience is generated. This mode of organizing experience is characterized by specific types of defense and forms of object relatedness, and a quality of anxiety and degree of subjectivity, that are described and clinically illustrated in greater detail in this chapter.

The state of being that is generated by this psychological organization stands in both a diachronic and a synchronic relationship to the paranoid-schizoid and depressive positions. Although the autistic-contiguous position has a period of primacy earlier than that of the two psychological organizations described by Klein, it coexists dialectically with the paranoid-schizoid and depressive positions from the beginning of psychological life. The concepts of the depressive, the paranoid-schizoid, and the autistic-contiguous positions constitute preserving and negating contexts for one another, just as the ideas of night and day, darkness and light, sound and silence, consciousness and unconsciousness each create, preserve, and negate the other. The delineation of the autistic-contiguous dimension of experience does not in any sense diminish the significance of the paranoid-schizoid and depressive dimensions. The present chapter represents an attempt to extend the concept of psychological "positions" or organizations to include the most primitive aspects of human experience.

Primitive Organization of Experience

The autistic-contiguous organization is associated with a specific mode of attributing meaning to experience in which raw sensory data are ordered by means of forming presymbolic connections between sensory impressions that come to constitute bounded surfaces. It is on these surfaces that the experience of self has its origins: "The ego [the "I"] is first and foremost a bodily ego. . . . (Freud, 1923, p. 26), i.e., the ego is ultimately derived from bodily sensations, chiefly from those springing from the surface of the body" (Freud, 1923, p. 26, footnote added in 1927).

I have retained the word *autistic* in the designation of the most primitive psychological organization despite the fact that the term is usually associated with a pathologically closed psychological system that I do not feel is characteristic of the normal autistic-contiguous mode. I have done so because I believe that pathological forms of autism involve hypertrophied versions of the types of defense, the method of attributing meaning to experience, and the mode of object relatedness characterizing the normal autistic-contiguous organization.

I believe the word *contiguous* is particularly apt in further naming this organization since, as is later discussed, the experience of surfaces touching one another is a principal medium through which connections are made and organization achieved in this psychological mode. The word *contiguous* thus provides the necessary antithesis to the connotations of isolation and disconnectedness carried by the word *autistic*.

This primitive psychological organization under normal circumstances contributes the barely perceptible background of sensory boundedness of all subsequent subjective states. When infantile anxiety is extreme (for constitutional and/or environmental reasons) the system of defenses characterizing this mode becomes hypertrophied and rigidified; this leads to a wide range of forms of pathological autism, ranging from pathological infantile autism to autistic features of patients who have in other ways achieved a predominantly neurotic psychological structure (cf. S. Klein, 1980; Tustin, 1986).

This conception of an autistic-contiguous position must be differentiated from Mahler's (1968) conception of "normal autism" (p. 7). She views the infant in the first months of life as existing in a "closed monadic system, self-sufficient in its hallucinatory wish fulfillment" (p. 7).[1] In contrast, I do not conceive of the autistic-contiguous position as a closed system in which the infant is isolated from, and unresponsive to, his object world. As will be discussed, object relations are experienced — in an autistic-contiguous mode — in terms of the sensory surfaces generated by the individual's interactions with his objects and by the sensory transformations occurring within the individual in the course of these interactions (cf. Bollas, 1979). The object (as sensory impression) is attributed meaning and responded to in an organized and organizing way, and in a way that involves a mutually transforming interplay of (nascent) self and object.

The observational data of Bower (1977), Brazelton (1981), Eimas (1975), Stern (1977, 1983, 1985), Trevarthan (1979), and others have provided powerful evidence for the capacity of the infant from the first days and weeks of life to perceive, make discriminations among, and respond to external objects in a way that is inferred to reflect the infant's (at least sporadic) awareness of externality. (I have elsewhere discussed central features of this body of data [Ogden, 1984].) Ordinarily, the interplay of the experience of oneness and that of separateness within the early mother–infant relationship makes tolerable the infant's moments of awareness of his separateness. The normal elaboration of the autistic-contiguous organization depends upon the capacity of the mother and infant to generate forms of sensory experi-

---

[1]Stern (1985) reports that Mahler near the end of her life expanded her conception of the earliest period of development to include greater recognition of the infant's awareness of and responsiveness to his human and nonhuman environment.

ence that "heal" or "make bearable" the awareness of the separateness that is an intrinsic component of early infantile experience (Tustin, 1986). When the mother–infant dyad is unable to function in a way that provides the infant a healing sensory experience, the holes in the fabric of the "emergent self" (Stern, 1985) become a source of unbearable "awareness of bodily separateness [which results in] an agony of consciousness" (Tustin, 1986, p. 43). Under such circumstances, the infant's development is skewed in the direction of pathological autism that involves the creation of a state of psychological deadness, which Meltzer and colleagues (1975) compares to the "absence" in a *petit mal* seizure and which I (Ogden, 1980) have described as a state of "non-experience," a state in which there is a cessation or paralysis of the process of attributing meaning to experience.

The Nature of Sensation-Dominated Experience

In an autistic-contiguous mode, it is experiences of sensation, particularly at the skin surface, that are the principal media for the creation of psychological meaning and the rudiments of the experience of self. Sensory contiguity of skin surface, along with the element of rhythmicity, are basic to the most fundamental set of infantile object relations: the infant's experience of being held, nursed, and spoken to by the mother. These early experiences are object-related in a specific sense of the word that is related to the nature of subjectivity in the autistic-contiguous position. In previous contributions (Ogden, 1986; see also Chapter 2), I have discussed Klein's concept of the depressive position as a psychological organization in which there is an interpreting subject mediating between symbol and symbolized, mediating between oneself and one's lived experience. In a paranoid-schizoid mode, there is very little sense of a mediating, interpreting "I"; instead, the self is to a large extent a self-as-object, a self that only minimally experiences itself as the author of its own thoughts, feelings, sensations, and perceptions. Instead, in a paranoid-schizoid mode, the individual experiences himself as buffeted by thoughts, feelings, and sensations as if they were forces or things that simply happen.

The nature of one's relationship to one's objects is determined to a large degree by the nature of the subjectivity (the form of "I-ness") that constitutes the context for those object relations. In the autistic-contiguous position, the relationship to objects is one in which the organization of a rudimentary sense of "I-ness" arises from relationships of sensory contiguity (i.e., *touching*) that over time generate the sense of a bounded sensory surface on which one's experience occurs (the beginnings of the feeling of "a place where one lives" [Winnicott, 1971a]). Examples of boundedness generated from relationships of contiguity include the sense of shape created by the impression of the infant's skin surface when he rests his cheek against the mother's breast; the sense of the continuity and predictability of shape derived from the rhythmicity and regularity of the infant's sucking activity (in the context of a maternally provided holding environment); the rhythm of the "dialogue" of cooing engaged in by mother and infant; the feeling of edgedness generated by the infant's pressing his gums tightly on the mother's nipple or finger.

The rudimentary beginnings of subjectivity in the autistic-contiguous position must be described from the perspective of two vertices simultaneously. On the one hand, the infant and mother are one: "There is no such thing as an infant" (Winnicott, 1960a, footnote on p. 39). From this perspective the infant's subjectivity can be thought of as being held in trust by the mother (more accurately, by the aspect of the mother–infant that an outside observer would view as the mother). At the same time, from another perspective, the infant and mother are never absolutely at one, and the infant's subjectivity in the autistic-contiguous position can be thought of as an extremely subtle, non-self-reflective sense of "going on being" (Winnicott, 1956) in which sensory need is in the process of acquiring features of subjective desire (the sensory-level beginnings of a subject wishing for something). Sensory experience in an autistic-contiguous mode has a quality of rhythmicity that is becoming continuity of being; it has boundedness that is the beginning of the experience of a place where one feels, thinks, and lives; it has such features as shape, hardness, coldness, warmth, and texture, that are the beginnings of the qualities of who one is.

Tustin (1980, 1984) has described two types of experience with objects that constitute important means of ordering and defining experience in the autistic-contiguous position. (These means of organizing and delineating experience are secondarily enlisted in the construction of psychological defense.) The first of these forms of relatedness to objects (which again only an outside observer would recognize as a relationship to an external object) is the creation of "autistic shapes" (1984).[2] Shapes generated in an autistic-contiguous mode

---

[2]Tustin (1980, 1984), following the lead of J. Anthony (1958), conceives of a phase of "normal autism" (which she more recently has

must be distinguished from what we ordinarily think of as the shape of an object. These early shapes are "'felt' shapes" (Tustin, 1986, p. 280) arising from the experience of soft touching of surfaces, which makes a sensory impression. The experience of shape in an autistic-contiguous mode does not involve the conception of the "objectness" or "thingness" of that which is being felt. As Tustin (1984) puts it, we can attempt to create for ourselves the experience of an autistic shape if we reduce the chair we are sitting on to the sensation it makes on our buttocks. From this perspective there is no sense of the chair as an object aside from the sensation that is generated. The "shape" of that impression is idiosyncratic to each of us, and changes as we shift in our seats.

For the infant, the objects generating shapes in an autistic-contiguous mode include the soft parts of his own body and the body of the mother as well as soft bodily substances (including saliva, urine, and feces). Experiences of shape in an autistic-contiguous mode contribute to the sense of cohesion of self and also to the experience of perception of what is becoming the object. Much later in development, words like "comfort," "soothing," "safety," "connectedness," "holding," "cuddling," and "gentleness" will be attached to the experience of shapes in an autistic-contiguous mode.

A second form of very early definition of sensory experience described by Tustin (1980), the experience of

---

designated the "auto-sensuous" [1986] phase of development). In this phase, the infant makes use of "shapes" in a way that resembles the shapes utilized by autistic children; however, the normal infantile utilization of shapes is not nearly as extensive or rigid, and does not serve to cut off relations with external objects, as is the case in pathological autism.

"autistic objects," stands in marked contrast to the experience of autistic shapes. An autistic object is the experience of a hard, angular sensory surface that is created when an object is pressed hard against the infant's skin. In this form of experience, the individual experiences his surface (which in a sense is all there is of him) as a hard crust or armor that protects him against unspeakable dangers that only later will be given names. An autistic object is a safety-generating sensory impression of edgedness that defines, delineates, and protects one's otherwise exposed and vulnerable surface. As experience is increasingly generated in paranoid-schizoid and depressive modes, words like "armor," "shell," "crust," "danger," "attack," "separateness," "otherness," "invasion," "rigidity," "impenetrability," and "repulsion" are attached to the quality of sensory impressions created by autistic objects.

I worked for many years in intensive psychotherapy with a congenitally blind schizophrenic adolescent named Robert (see Ogden, 1982a, for an extended discussion of this case). In the initial years of this work, which began when the patient was 19 years old, he spoke very little. The patient said that he was terrified of the millions of spiders that were all over the floor, his food, and his body. He felt that they were crawling in and out of all his bodily openings including his eyes, mouth, ears, nose, anus, and penis as well as the pores of his skin. He would sit in my office trembling with his eyes rolled back into their sockets so that only the sclerae were visible.

According to the history given by the patient's parents, siblings, and other relatives, Robert's mother's handling of him as an infant was characterized by unpredictable shifts from smothering overinvolvement to extremes of hatred for him. He was left alone in a mobile crib for hours. Robert would stand up in the crib, holding onto the bar forming its upper edge, and would propel himself around the room by rhythmically banging his head against the bar. His mother told me that he had seemed oblivious to the pain and that she had been horrified by his "demoniacal willfulness."

In the period of treatment that I will be focusing upon here, Robert refused to bathe despite every act of prodding, cajoling, bribing, and threatening that the nursing staff could devise. (He was hospitalized for the initial year of treatment.) He rarely changed his clothes even to sleep, and his hair was a mass of greasy clumps.

Robert developed an intense bodily odor that silently accompanied him and that lingered for hours following his departure from my office. He would lie back in the soft chair in my consulting room with his greasy hair on the hard, padded back of the chair. The aspect of the transference–countertransference interaction that I was most aware of at the time was the way in which I felt invaded by this patient. When he left my office, I could not feel that I had a respite from him. I felt as if he had managed, in a literal way, to get inside of me—to get under my skin—by means of his odor that was saturating my furniture (with which I had become closely identified). I eventually understood these feelings as my response to (unconscious participation in) a projective identification in which the patient was engendering in me his own feelings of being painfully and unwillingly infiltrated by his internal object mother.

In retrospect I feel that I did not give sufficient weight to an aspect of the experience to which the patient was unconsciously directing my attention.

When I asked Robert what it was about showering that most frightened him, he said, "the drain." I now feel that I understand in a fuller way than I did at the time that Robert was terrified of dissolving and literally going down the drain. Thus he attempted to ground himself in the sensation of his own distinct bodily odor, which was of particular importance to him in the absence of the capacity to form well-defined visual images. His odor constituted a comforting autistic shape that helped him to create a place in which he could feel (through his bodily sensations) that he existed. His trembling gave him a heightened sense of his skin; his rolling of his eyes back into the vault of his skull insulated him from the blurred, edgeless shadows that he perceived visually. (Years later he told me that these shadows were "worse than seeing nothing at all" because they made him feel as if he were drowning.)

The patient's insistence on holding his head against the back edge of my chair served to provide some degree of boundedness for him. In early childhood, Robert had in a similar way desperately attempted to repair a failing sense of self-cohesiveness through his banging of his head against the hard edge of his crib in response to the disintegrative effect of long periods of disconnectedness from his mother. This early "relationship" to hardness represents a form of pathological use of an autistic object as a substitute for a healing relationship with an actual person. The rhythmic component of the head-banging and of the crib's motion can be viewed as an effort at self-soothing through the use of an autistic shape.

From this perspective, Robert's insistence on not bathing is more fully understandable. The loss of his odor would have been equivalent to the loss of himself.

His odor provided the rudiments of being someone
(someone who had a particular odor), being somewhere
(somewhere in which he could perceive his odor), and
being something for another person (a person who
could smell him, be infused by him, and remember
him). The use of odor as an autistic shape can in this
case be viewed as nonpathological to the extent that it
existed as a part of the transference–countertransference relationship that was to a large degree aimed at
the establishment of an object relationship of contiguity (the "touch" of odor), and was not simply an
effort at creating a substitute for the object.

Autistic-Contiguous Experience and Pathological Autism

Although pathological autism can be thought of as constituting an "asymbolic" realm, the normal autistic-
contiguous mode is "presymbolic" in that the sensory-
based units of experience being organized are
preparatory for the creation of symbols mediated by
experience of transitional phenomena (Winnicott, 1951).
The developmental directionality of this process stands in
contrast to the static nature of asymbolic experience in
pathological autism, wherein the effort is to maintain a
perfectly insulated closed system (in which sensory experience does not lead anywhere except back to itself).
Pathological autism aims at the absolute elimination of
the unknown and the unpredictable.

The machinelike predictability of experiences with
pathological autistic shapes and objects substitutes for
experiences with inevitably imperfect and not entirely

predictable human beings. No person can compete with the capacity of never-changing autistic shapes and objects to provide absolutely reliable comfort and protection.

Experience at the skin surface is critically important during infancy in that it constitutes an arena where there is a convergence of the infant's idiosyncratic, presymbolic world of sensory impressions, and the interpersonal world made up of objects that — as viewed by an outside observer — have an existence separate from the infant and outside of his omnipotent control. It is on this stage that the infant will either elaborate a way of being in the world in relation to the mother and the rest of the object world, or will elaborate sensory-dominated ways of being (more accurately a way of *not-being*) that are designed to insulate a potential self (that never comes into being) from all that lies outside of his sensory-dominated world. To the extent that the bodily system is closed off from mutually transforming experiences with human beings, there is an absence of "potential space" (Winnicott, 1971a; see also Ogden, 1985b, 1986) between oneself and the other (a potential psychological space between self-experience and sensory perception). This closed bodily world is a world without room in which to create a distinction between symbol and symbolized, and therefore a world in which there is no possibility for the coming into being of an interpreting subject; it is a world in which there is no psychological space between the infant and the mother in which transitional phenomena might be created/discovered.

The syndrome of pathological infantile rumination is paradigmatic of the self-enclosed circularity of the pathological autistic process:

Rumination or merycism . . . [is] the active bringing into the mouth of swallowed food which has already reached the stomach and which may have started to undergo the process of digestion. . . . The food may be partially reswallowed, partially lost, with serious consequences for the infant's nutrition. Unlike regurgitation, where the food runs out of the infant's mouth without any effort, in rumination there are complex and purposeful preparatory movements particularly of the tongue and of the abdominal muscles. In some cases the hard palate is stimulated by fingers in the mouth. When the efforts become successful and the milk appears on the back of the pharynx, the child's face is pervaded by an ecstatic expression. [Gaddini and Gaddini, 1959, p. 166]

In infantile rumination, the beginnings of the awareness of otherness (through the feeding interaction) is short-circuited by the infant's appropriating to himself the entire feeding situation and then engaging in a tightly closed auto-sensory cycle of creating his food (more accurately, creating his autistic shapes). These autistic shapes then substitute for the mother, thus transforming the feeding experience from an avenue toward increasingly mature object relatedness, into a pathway leading to objectless "self-sufficiency" (in which there is no self).

In the analytic setting, one form of equivalent of merycism can be seen in patients who take the analysis into themselves. Instead of internalizing an analytic space in which one thinks and feels one's thoughts, feelings, and sensations, such patients present a caricature of analysis in which rumination and imitation substitute for an analytic process. The analyst's role has been entirely co-opted. Such patients often present the unconscious phantasy of having "raised themselves" by taking into themselves the functions of both parent and child, thus replacing genuine object relatedness with an inner world of phantasied object relations and experiences with autistic shapes and objects.

Mrs. M., a 62-year-old widow whom I saw in intensive psychotherapy for eight years, had originally been referred to me by her internist after a suicide attempt. She had used a razor to carefully make deep incisions across her wrists, arms, legs, and ankles. She then got into a tub filled with warm water and patiently waited for over three hours to bleed to death. After lapsing into a coma, she was discovered by a cleaning-woman. While waiting to die, she had felt the relief of the end of decades of oppressive obsessive-compulsive rituals.

Speaking in clipped sentences and almost exclusively in response to direct questions, Mrs. M. told me that she would stand for hours in front of one door or another in her apartment before she would allow herself to go through it while she attempted to "get a thought right." "Getting a thought right" involved generating for herself a perfect mental re-creation of some experience from her past, including all of its sensory features. For years (including the initial years of the therapy), this effort was focused on an attempt to re-experience the taste of the first sip of a cold glass of wine that the patient had tasted early in the relationship with her husband some thirty-eight years before. She could not allow herself to open any door of her apartment, whether to go into the next room or out into the hallway, until she had successfully completed this task. She compared getting a thought right to having an orgasm; it was a fitting together of different sensations and rhythms in a very specific way. For years, such obsessive-compulsive activity filled virtually every moment of Mrs. M.'s life. This activity was understood in the course of the therapy as providing a form of comfort that was both nightmarishly tyrannizing and yet life-sustaining.

The patient was terrified of the disruption of her bodily rhythms, particularly her breathing. During her obsessional marathons, Mrs. M. felt terrified of suffocating and felt that she would not be able to resume breathing normally until she "got the thought right." In the meantime, she felt that she had to take over the process of breathing with conscious control; she could never feel that her breathing was natural, automatic, and sufficient. The patient was convinced that if she forgot to breathe she would suffocate.

Although Mrs. M. highly valued the therapy and was never late to her daily meetings with me, she found it extremely painful when I spoke because this interfered with her ability to concentrate. The experience of being with this patient was quite different from that of being with a silent patient for whom one feels one is providing a "holding environment" (Winnicott, 1960a). Instead, I generally felt useless. Mrs. M. could and did ruminate at home in precisely the way she was doing with me. If anything, I seemed to make things worse for her by placing an additional demand on her — the demand that she felt from me to be acknowledged and made use of as a human being and as a therapist. I said to her in small bits in the second year of our work that I assumed that my own wishes to be experienced by her as human were a reflection of an aspect of herself, but that she did not at the moment feel she could afford this complicated luxury since she was so fully involved in fighting for her life. She would look at me and nod as if to say, "I understand what you said, but I'm too busy to talk now," and then would continue with her task.

Occasionally she would breathe a sigh of relief,

glance at me, nod her head and smile in a joyless way, saying, "I got it right." She would then seem to relax and stare at me as if she were coming out of anesthesia, looking to see who it was that had been with her during her ordeal. She would then begin to brace herself for the inevitable recurrence of the need to chase another thought so that even these interim periods were far from relaxed.

Mrs. M. was able to offer fragments of history during the brief periods of respite before becoming fully re-immersed in her rumination. I learned that she had deeply loved and admired her husband, a professor twenty years her senior, and that they had lived very happily together during their twenty-two years of marriage. It was eight years after his death that the patient attempted suicide.

Dr. and Mrs. M. had had a large photograph collection of their lives together which the patient impulsively threw out after Dr. M. died, "because it was too much at loose ends to pack." (It pained me to hear her speak of this since it felt as if she had brutally sliced out a terribly important part of herself in this impulsive act.) Mrs. M. had saved only one picture from that collection, a photo of herself and her husband with a "real lion" between whose open jaws her husband was holding his hand.

Mrs. M.'s mother had been a psychotic actress who believed that she could read her daughter's mind and knew what she was thinking better than her daughter herself did. Mrs. M. as a child was used as a prop in her mother's delusional dramas. The child kept important trinkets and ticket stubs in a Chinese box given to her by her grandmother. In a fit of rage about the secretive nature of this child, the mother (when the patient was 10 years old) threw the box away while the patient was at school. When Mrs. M. told me this, I said that I thought I finally was beginning to understand something of the meaning of her throwing her photographs away; one's most precious possessions are only safe if they are inside of you.

Over time, I realized that this interpretation was incomplete in an important way. Mrs. M. often indicated that she had practically no sense of an internal space within which to keep anything. She told me, "I have no insides. I had a hysterectomy when I was 45."

I later said to her that I thought that when she felt she had no safe place in her to keep the people and things that were most important to her, she felt that she had to find a way to freeze time. "Getting a thought right" about the taste of the wine was not an attempt to remember something. To remember would be much too painful because she would then know that the moment was over. I said she gave me the feeling that she was attempting to become timeless and placeless — that she could enter the sensation, the taste, and become it. Everything would be there that she needed. It was only there that she could relax. (The photograph of her husband holding his hand between the lion's open jaws must also have captured for Mrs. M. a feeling that time could really be frozen.)

Mrs. M.'s ruminative symptoms had not begun with her husband's death. From adolescence and before she had devoted her life to endless attempts at living in a realm of timeless sensations. In the therapy, I initially attempted to understand the meaning of the choice of each sensation, but over time I realized that this patient's psychological world was not composed of accretions of meaning; rather, she lived in a world of timeless sensory experience that was neither internal nor external. The ruminative activity was the essence of pure, unchanging sensation. Mrs. M.'s suicide attempt and her longing for death represented her hope that if this timeless state could not be achieved in life, perhaps it could be achieved in death.

The early relationship between Mrs. M. and her mother had not resulted in the creation of a gradual internalization of a holding environment. Instead, Mrs. M. had defensively attempted to create a substitute for such an environment. She could not take for granted that the rhythm of her breathing would sustain itself and her without her consciously willing it. The patient's life was devoted to creating a substitute for the space between mother and infant in which the infant ordinarily finds a place to live between self and other. In the absence of such a space (symbolized by the box in which the patient had attempted to store precious bits of herself and her relations to external objects), Mrs. M. attempted to become sensation itself.

In the course of eight years of therapy, Mrs. M. began to be able to live for extended periods of time in a state of mind relatively free of her obsessive ruminations. While this was occurring, I increasingly felt that I was perceiving the faint glimmer of a living human being in the room with me. At times I saw brief glimpses of a little girl capable of some joy as Mrs. M. laughed about some humorous event in her life with her husband or about something I had said that she found funny. It was with a mixture of sadness and a vicarious sense of relief that I received a phone call I had been half expecting from the moment I met Mrs. M.: she had been brought to the hospital after a massive stroke and died soon afterward.

I view the autistic-contiguous mode as an important dimension of all obsessive-compulsive defenses, and believe that these defenses always entail the construction of a tightly ordered sensory containment of experience that is never simply a symbolic, ideational ordering of experience designed to ward off, control, and express conflicted unconscious anal-erotic wishes and fears. This form of defense regularly serves to plug sensorially experienced holes in the individual's sense of self through which the patient fears and *feels* (in the most concrete sensory way) that not only ideas, but actual bodily contents, will leak. Obsessive-compulsive symptoms and defenses have their origins in the infant's earliest efforts at ordering and creating a sense of boundedness for his sensory experience. Very early on, such efforts at organization and definition come to be utilized in the service of warding off anxiety related to the disruption of the sensory-dominated, rudimentary sense of self.

The Nature of Autistic-Contiguous Anxiety

Each of the three basic psychological organizations (the autistic-contiguous, the paranoid-schizoid and the depressive) is associated with its own characteristic form of anxiety. In each case, the nature of the anxiety is related to the experience of disconnectedness (dis-integration) within that mode of experience, whether it be the disruption of whole object relations in the depressive position, the fragmentation of parts of self and object in the paranoid-schizoid position, or the disruption of sensory cohesion and boundedness in the autistic-contiguous position.

Depressive anxiety involves the fear that one has in

fact or in phantasy harmed or driven away a person whom one loves; anxiety in a paranoid-schizoid mode is at core a sense of impending annihilation which is experienced in the form of fragmenting attacks on the self and on one's objects; autistic-contiguous anxiety involves the experience of impending disintegration of one's sensory surface or one's "rhythm of safety" (Tustin, 1986), resulting in the feeling of leaking, dissolving, disappearing, or falling into shapeless unbounded space (cf. Bick, 1968; E. Gaddini, 1987; Rosenfeld, 1984).

Common manifestations of autistic-contiguous anxiety include terrifying feelings that one is rotting; the sensation that one's sphincters and other means of containing bodily contents are failing and that one's saliva, tears, urine, feces, blood, menstrual fluids, and so forth are leaking; fear that one is falling–for example, anxiety connected with falling asleep for fear that one will fall into endless, shapeless space. Patients experiencing this form of insomnia often attempt to relieve their anxiety (their fear of "falling asleep") by tightly surrounding themselves with blankets and pillows, keeping bright lights on in their bedrooms or playing familiar music all night.

Ms. K., a 25-year-old graduate student, began therapy because of her terror of the fog and of the sound of the ocean. The fog was frighteningly suffocating: "You can't see the horizon." The patient was terrified of "going crazy" and of being unaware that it was happening; she frequently beseeched the therapist to inform her if the therapist should sense that the patient was losing touch with reality.

When Ms. K. was 4 months old, her mother

contracted spinal meningitis and was hospitalized for
fourteen months. From the time the mother returned
home, she tyrannically ruled the house from the metal
wheelchair to which she was confined. The patient's
earliest memory (which seemed to her as much a dream
as a memory) was of reaching out to her mother in the
wheel chair and being pushed away by her. At the same
moment, the patient, in this memory, looked out of the
window and saw a small girl falling through the ice on
the pond that was located just behind the patient's
house. Mrs. K. said to her daughter, "You'd better go
save her."

I view this "memory" as a vivid representation of the
patient's experience of falling through the containing
surface of self (initially created in the interaction of
mother and infant). Ms. K. is both the small child falling
through the ice and the older child who must try to pull
the younger one out of the hole before she drowns. The
metallic, wheelchair–mother is felt to be incapable of
saving the child and in fact seems to be the one who is
unconsciously being blamed for the little girl's fall
through the hole (the mother's pushing Ms. K. away).

The ocean and the fog came to be experienced by
Ms. K. as the ever-present danger of annihilating shapelessness into which she might fall. Because of the tenu-
ousness of the patient's sense of cohesiveness of self, she
lived in constant fear of "going crazy" (losing "touch" with
reality in a literal, sensory way). The patient lacked the
feeling of sensory groundedness that is ordinarily provided by the interpersonal "touch" of our shared sensory
experience of the world, which heavily contributes to our
sense of being sane.

Autistic-Contiguous Modes of Defense

Defenses generated in an autistic-contiguous mode are directed at re-establishment of the continuity of the bounded sensory surface and of the ordered rhythmicity upon which the early integrity of self rests. Within the analytic hour, patients spanning the full range of psychological maturity commonly attempt to reconstitute a sensory "floor" (Grotstein, 1987) of experience by means of activities like hair twirling or foot tapping (even while lying on the couch); stroking of the lips, cheek, or ear lobe; humming, intoning, picturing or repeating series of numbers, focusing on symmetrical geometric shapes on the ceiling or wall, or using a finger to trace shapes on the wall next to the couch. Such activities can be thought of as self-soothing uses of autistic shapes.

Between analytic hours, patients commonly attempt to maintain or re-establish a failing sense of bodily cohesion by means of rhythmic muscular activities including long periods of bicycle riding, jogging, lap swimming, and the like; eating and purging rituals; rocking (sometimes in a rocking chair); head banging (often against a pillow); riding buses and subways or driving a car for hours; maintaining and continually working on ("perfecting") a system of numbers or geometric shapes in one's head or in computer programs; and so on. The absolute regularity of these activities is so essential to the process of allaying anxiety that the individual cannot or will not allow any other activity to take precedence over them.

Bick (1968, 1986) uses the phrase "second skin formation" to describe the way in which the individual attempts to create a substitute for a deteriorating sense of the cohesiveness of skin surface. Often the individual attempts to use the sensory experience of adhering to the surface of the object in order to resurrect the integrity of his own surface.

Meltzer and colleagues (1975) have introduced the term *adhesive identification* to refer to the defensive adherence to the object in the service of allaying the anxiety of disintegration. Imitation and mimicry, for instance, are utilized in an effort to make use of the surface of the object as if it were one's own. In an autistic-contiguous mode, one attempts to defend against the anxiety of disintegration by sticking bits of the surface of the object to one's own failing surface.

Mrs. R., in a regressed phase of her analysis, would spend hours at a time picking at her face. She suffered from severe insomnia in large part due to a fear of nightmares that she could not recall. Over time her face became covered with scabs, and she picked at these. As this "picking" was occurring in the analytic hours, the patient was clearly in a painfully anxious state although she said that she had "absolutely no thoughts."

Mrs. R. took bits of tissue from the Kleenex box next to the couch and stuck them to the lesions she was creating on her face. (She would also take extra pieces of these tissues home with her at the end of the hour.) It did not seem to me that either self-destructive wishes or displaced hostility toward me was at the core of this activity at this point in the analysis. I told her that I thought she must feel as if she were without skin; that she did not sleep because when she was asleep she must feel psychologically defenseless to the danger of nightmares. I said that I could understand her attempt to cover herself with my skin (tissues) since this seemed to make her feel a little less raw.

In the hour following this intervention, Mrs. R. fell asleep and slept for almost the entire session until I woke her to tell her that our time was up. During the next meeting, the patient said that even though she had not had a blanket while sleeping in my office, she had the distinct feeling when recalling that session that she had been sleeping under some sort of cover. Mrs. R.'s capacity to sleep during her session represented an expanded and more fully symbolic use of me as a second skin. She had utilized me and the analytic setting as a symbolic and yet tangibly felt medium in which to wrap herself. She had thus felt sufficiently covered and held together to safely sleep.

Before concluding this section, I would like to briefly mention two forms of symptomatology in which the concept of autistic-contiguous modes of defense must supplement understandings formulated in terms of defenses erected to deal with anxiety resulting from conflicted sexual and aggressive wishes. First, compulsive masturbation often serves the purpose of creating a heightened experience of a sensory surface in order to ward off feelings of loss of sensory cohesion. For example, a female patient would masturbate for hours each day without conscious sexual fantasy. Orgasm was not the goal. When orgasm did occur, it was experienced as an unwelcome "anticlimax" which ended the only part of the patient's day during which she felt "alive and in one piece."

Secondly, painful, anxiety-producing procrastination also often serves the purpose of generating a palpable sensory edge against which the patient attempts to define himself. The "deadline" is elevated to the position of a continually felt pressure in the patient's emotional life that can be a felt presence at every moment, whether or not the patient is consciously focused upon it. These patients describe the anxiety of the approaching deadline as a pressure that they hate, and yet at the same time continually seem to create for themselves: "A due date is something to push up against like a wall in front of me."

Under such circumstances, a deadline that is finally met does not usually produce more than a sense of momentary relief, and instead often throws the patient into a state of panic. Very frequently such patients become physically ill once the task has been completed (usually at the last possible moment prior to the deadline), experiencing such symptoms as migraine headaches, dermatitis, or somatic delusions. Such symptoms can be understood as substitute efforts at maintaining a sensory surface in the absence of the containing pressure of the deadline.

Internalization in the Autistic-Contiguous Position

As previously mentioned, in a psychological field in which the individual has little if any sense of internal space, the concept of internalization becomes virtually meaningless; this is especially true when the idea of internalization (including identification and introjection) is linked to the notion of conscious and unconscious fantasies about taking parts or all of another person into oneself. Nonetheless, psychological change can result from experience with external objects in an autistic-contiguous mode; such change is mediated in part by the process of imitation. In autistic-contiguous forms of imitation, the individual experiences a change in the shape of his surface as a result of the influence of his relations with external objects. At times, imitation is one of the few ways the individual has of holding onto attributes of the object, in the absence of the experience of having an inner space in which the other person's qualities or parts can in phantasy be stored (cf. E. Gaddini, 1969). Since in an autistic-contiguous mode the feeling and phantasy of being entered is synonymous with being torn or punctured, imitation allows the influence of the other to be carried on one's surface. In pathological autism this sometimes manifests itself as echolalia or as an endless repetition of a phrase or a word uttered by another person.[3]

Imitation as a method of achieving a degree of cohesiveness of self must be distinguished from Winnicott's (1963b) concept of a False Self personality organization. There is nothing false about autistic-contiguous imitation in that it does not stand in contrast to, or serve to disguise or protect, something truer or more genuine within: there *is* no within or without. In an autistic-contiguous mode, one is one's surface, and therefore the act of imitation is an effort at becoming or

----

[3]Awareness of the importance of the role of imitation in normal early development — prior to the development of "internalization processes" — is reflected in Fenichel's (1945) comment (later elaborated upon by E. Gaddini [1969, 1987] and Schafer [1968]) that early on, imitation represents an important aspect of sensory perception. One perceives the other by experiencing the other's qualities *through one's own bodily sensations,* in the process of creating (shaping) oneself in the likeness of the other.

repairing a cohesive surface on which a locus of self can develop.

Imitation serves not only as a form of perception, a defense, and a way of "holding onto" (being shaped by) the other, it serves also as an important form of object relatedness in an autistic-contiguous mode.

In a previous paper (1980), I described aspects of my work with a hospitalized chronically schizophrenic patient who for years lived in a world so stripped of meaning that people and things were treated by him as completely interchangeable. Phil seemed psychologically dead as he lay on the floor of my office or was escorted from one hospital "activity" to another. The initial form of contact that he made with me in the therapy was by imitating my posture, my tone of voice, my every gesture, every word I spoke, and every facial expression I made. Rather than celebrating this as his entry into the land of the living, I experienced it at the time as an attack on my ability to feel alive. I felt as if my spontaneity was being tyrannically drained out of me. Nothing I did felt natural.

At that time I understood this as a form of projective identification (cf. Ogden, 1979, 1982b, 1983), in which the patient was engendering in me (communicating to me) his own feelings of lifelessness and incapacity for spontaneity as well as his inability to feel alive in any way. However, I did not at the time sufficiently understand the phenomena that I am referring to here as autistic-contiguous to appreciate the nature of the affection in the patient's imitation of me. He was using me as a second skin or container within which he was experimenting in a primitive way with what it might feel like to be alive. He was paying me a very great compliment indeed by indicating that it was to be my skin in which he would conduct this experiment.

Winnicott (1965), in a letter to Michael Fordham, addressed—from the perspective of the treatment of an autistic child—the role of imitation as a primitive form of object relatedness.

> I know an autistic child who is treated by very clever interpretations and who has done moderately well. What started off the treatment was, however, something which the first analyst did, and it is strange that I have never been able to get the second analyst to acknowledge the importance of what I will describe. The first analyst, Dr. Mida Hall, died. Dr. Hall found this boy who had gone autistic after being normal and sat in the room with him and established a communication by doing everything that this boy did. He would sit still for a quarter of an hour and then move his foot a little; she would move her foot. His finger would move and she would imitate, and this went on for a long time. Out of these beginnings everything showed signs of developing until she died. If I could have got the clever analyst to join on to all this I think we might by now have had something like a cure instead of having to put up with one of those maddening cases where a lot of good work has been done and everybody is very pleased but the child is not satisfactory. [Winnicott, 1965, pp. 150–151]

Imitation in an autistic-contiguous mode is by no means restricted to patients suffering from pathological childhood autism, borderline conditions, and schizophrenia. It is very common for a therapist early in training to attempt to imitate his supervisors or his own therapist in an attempt to hide from himself the absence of his own identity as a therapist. One such therapist described this experience as "using the skin of the supervisor" when he was with his patients. This "skin" was felt to be "stripped off" when a second supervisor was critical of this student's work, leading the trainee to feel painfully "raw." He would then immediately attempt to "take on the skin of the second supervisor." In therapy, this patient imitated his own patients by presenting their difficulties as his own, thus defending against his awareness of the feeling that he did not have a voice of his own with which to speak. Instead, the patient desperately attempted to get the therapist to make interpretations and give advice which would serve as substitutes for the patient's own thoughts and feelings, as well as a substitute for a voice that he could feel was his own.

Autistic-Contiguous Anxiety and the Binding Power of Symbols

As has been discussed in this and the previous chapter, each of the three modes of generating experience — the depressive, the paranoid-schizoid, and the autistic-contiguous — represents a pole of a dialectical process between which experience is generated. Psychopathology can be thought of as a collapse of the generative dialectical interplay of modes of experience (cf. Ogden, 1985b, 1986). Collapse in the direction of an autistic-contiguous mode results in a tyrannizing imprisonment in a closed system of bodily sensations that precludes the development of "potential space" (Winnicott, 1971a). Collapse in

the direction of a paranoid-schizoid mode results in a
sense of entrapment in a world of things-in-themselves
wherein one does not experience oneself as the author of
one's own thoughts and feelings; rather, thoughts, feelings, and sensations are experienced as objects or forces
bombarding, entering into, or propelled from oneself.
Collapse in the direction of a depressive mode results in
the experience of a subject alienated from his bodily
sensations and from the immediacy and spontaneity of
lived experience.

   A discussion of the diversity and complexity of the
dialectical interplay of the depressive, the paranoid-
schizoid and the autistic-contiguous modes was begun in
the previous chapter. I would like to offer some additional
observations here about an aspect of this interplay of
modes. There is a form of interpenetration of autistic-
contiguous and depressive modes through which the
sensory boundedness of the autistic-contiguous position,
and the capacity for symbol formation, historicity, and
subjectivity of the depressive position, together contribute to the creation of a whole that is larger than the
sum of its parts. In the absence of this mutually generative interplay, specific forms of psychopathology are
generated. It is to these types of pathology that I shall
now turn the focus of discussion.

   Disconnectedness of the depressive mode from the
autistic-contiguous mode leads to psychological states in
which the individual becomes either alienated from or
entrapped in sensory experience. In the former case, the
individual defensively attempts to use ideas, words, and
other forms of *symbol formation proper* (Segal, 1957) as
substitutes for an internal sensory groundedness in sensation-dominated experience. This form of alienation from

one's sensory experience is illustrated in the following clinical example.

Mr. D., an extremely bright graduate student in philosophy, began analysis at the age of 25. He told me that he did not know what it meant to feel sexual desire. The patient had, of course, heard other people describe such feelings, but he did not know from his own experience what it felt like to be sexually excited. He could, with effort, spend time with and converse with fellow students of both sexes, but he did not feel that anything he did was "natural." In fact, nothing in his life felt natural with the exception of the time he spent kayaking during which he could completely relax and "flow with the river" in an unself-conscious way.

In this case, neither the autistic-contiguous mode nor the depressive mode was absent, but each had become disconnected from the other. Mr. D. perpetually felt like a visitor. Traveling in an airplane provided another of the rare occasions during which he could relax: he knew he did not fit in the place he had left and he knew he would not fit in the place to which he was going, but at least for the duration of the flight he felt less painfully out of place. It is only in the generative interplay of the autistic-contiguous and the depressive modes of generating experience that one creates the feeling that one has a place of one's own in the "order of things," and can do things in a way that feels natural.

In the case of Mr. D., the collapse of the dialectical interplay of the autistic-contiguous and the depressive modes—a collapse in his case in the direction of the depressive—led to a rigidly defensive and im-

poverished psychological state that might be thought of
as a schizoid state (Fairbairn, 1940) or a "dis-affected
state" (McDougall, 1984). Perhaps Mr. D.'s psychological state might be best described as a "de-sensate state."

The dialectic of the autistic-contiguous and the
depressive modes of generating experience may also
collapse in the direction of the autistic-contiguous,
leading to a feeling of entrapment in a world of sensation
that is almost completely unmediated and undefined by
symbols. Many years ago, I inadvertently stumbled upon
a way of creating for oneself this type of disconnection of
the autistic-contiguous mode from the depressive mode.
After dinner one night, while I was still sitting at the
dining-room table, it suddenly occurred to me how
strange it was that the thing called a napkin was named by
the conjunction of the sounds "nap" and "kin." I repeated
the two sounds over and over until I began to get the very
frightening feeling that these sounds had no connection at
all with this thing that I was looking at. I could not get
these sounds to naturally "mean" the thing that they had
meant only minutes before. The link was broken, and, to
my horror, could not be mended simply by an act of will.
I imagined that I could, if I chose to, destroy the power of
any and all words to "mean" something if I thought about
them one at a time in this way. At that point, I had the
very disturbing feeling that I had discovered a way to
drive myself crazy. I imagined that all things in the world
could come to feel as disconnected as the napkin had
become for me now that it had been disconnected from
the word that had formerly named it. Further, I felt that
I could become utterly disconnected from the rest of the
world because all other people would still share in a
"natural" (i.e., a still meaningful) system of words. Such

is the nature of the beginnings of a collapse of the dialectic of experience in the direction of sensation-dominated experience that is unmediated by the use of symbols. It took some years before the word "napkin" re-entered my vocabulary in a fully unself-conscious way.

The fact that one's experience of self is powerfully rooted in the dialectical interplay of the sensory and the symbolic is often highly visible in psychoanalytic work with teachers and students of linguistics. These patients often experience anxiety states bordering on panic in association with the feeling that they are dissolving as they dismantle the binding power of language. This has in each case that I have encountered led to the patient's need to leave the field of linguistics at least temporarily.

Summary

In this chapter, the idea of an autistic-contiguous position has been proposed as a way of conceptualizing a psychological organization more primitive than either the paranoid-schizoid or the depressive position. The autistic-contiguous mode is conceptualized as a sensory-dominated, presymbolic mode of generating experience which provides a good measure of the boundedness of human experience, and the beginnings of a sense of the place where one's experience occurs. Anxiety in this mode consists of an unspeakable terror of the dissolution of boundedness resulting in feelings of leaking, falling, or dissolving into endless, shapeless space. Principal forms of defense, ways of organizing and defining experience, types of relatedness to objects, and avenues to psychological change in the autistic-contiguous position, have been discussed and clinically illustrated in this chapter.

4

The Schizoid Condition

> *. . . or music heard so deeply*
> *That it is not heard at all, but you are*
> *the music.*
>   T. S. Eliot, "The Dry Salvages"

It has been half a century since Fairbairn (1940) published his pioneering work, "Schizoid factors in the personality." I believe that most of what is presently understood about schizoid phenomena can be found in that classic paper and in the three that followed shortly thereafter (1941, 1943, 1944). However, developments in analytic thinking over the past twenty years require that we re-examine our conception of the schizoid personality. No longer is it possible to maintain the views of Fairbairn and later of Klein (1946), that the schizoid organization represents the most primitive human psychological organization. In the present chapter, I propose that autistic-contiguous phenomena can be thought of as the "underbelly"—or the primitive edge—of the schizoid personality organization.

I shall begin by delineating what it is that I have in mind when I refer to the schizoid condition. The initial picture that will be presented represents a condensation of my own interpretation of the work of Fairbairn and Klein. Although the metapsychologies of Fairbairn and Klein differ in fundamental ways, I have found that these analysts are in basic agreement with regard to the phenomenology of schizoid experience. This will be followed by a discussion of aspects of the work of Winnicott and Guntrip that address the schizoid condition. Finally, I shall discuss portions of the analysis of a schizoid patient in an effort to demonstrate the way in which analytic thinking about schizoid phenomena must incorporate an understanding of the nature of the interplay of autistic-contiguous and paranoid-schizoid modes of generating experience.

Schizoid Phenomena

The schizoid patient[1] to a large degree has retreated from object relations with whole external objects into an internal world comprised of conscious and unconscious

---

[1]The term *schizoid* is used in this chapter to refer to that aspect of all personalities that is organized around unconscious defensive attachment of aspects of the self to internal objects. When this universal dimension of the personality becomes hypertrophied for defensive purposes, it forms the basis for a range of types of psychopathology, including schizoid and narcissistic character disorders. Schizophrenia stands in marked contrast to the schizoid personality organization in that the former represents a fragmentation (disorganization) of the personality, whereas the latter represents a form of psychological cohesiveness based on stable (though often rigid) internal object relationships.

relations to internal objects. These phantasied object relations are conducted in a realm of omnipotent thought with heavy reliance on splitting and projective identification as modes of defense. It is a world of heroes and villains, of persecutors and victims; a world in which object ties are often addictive in nature, and loved objects are tantalizing and unattainable; a world in which introjects are omniscient and conduct unrelentingly critical narratives of one's phantasied and actual behavior. For this individual, external objects are so thoroughly eclipsed by transference projections of his internal object world that the qualities of the external object are barely discernible.

To the extent that the external world is blanketed in a shroud of transference projections, the individual is unable to learn from experience. The present is merely a re-enactment of the past using external objects as props for the re-creation of a timeless internal drama.[2] When an external object fails to conform to the unconscious script and direction of the patient, the use of denial, contempt, grandiosity, distortion of perception, and/or emotional withdrawal serve to reduce to a minimum the

---

[2]For Fairbairn (1944, 1946), the stability of unconscious attachments to internal objects is the principal source of the stability of the organization of the personality of every individual. Unconscious attachment to internal objects is the "glue" that holds together all personality organizations. The schizoid individual has "too much glue" in the sense that his internal attachments are so intense as to almost completely foreclose emotional involvement with external objects. However, in extreme cases, psychic energy is withdrawn not only from external object relations, but from internal object relations as well. The result is a catastrophic "loss of the ego" (Fairbairn 1941, p. 42)—in effect, a destruction of the schizoid ego organization and the onset of schizophrenic breakdown.

impact of the experience with the external object. As a result, the individual remains unchanged by his experience in the world. He unconsciously knows that he is an actor trapped in his own internal drama, and as a result experiences profound feelings of futility and emptiness.

The emptiness of the schizoid patient is not simply the emptiness of loneliness; it is also the emptiness of ungroundedness in anything outside of his own mind. It is the emptiness of a self that is imaginary because it is disconnected from intersubjective human experience, through which the self ordinarily acquires a sense of its own realness through recognition by the other (Habermas, 1968; Hegel, 1807; Kojève, 1934–1935). The schizoid patient is "occupied by," and preoccupied with, his internal object relationships; and yet these relationships are, in themselves, insubstantial, leading to a state of emotional impoverishment. The situation is analogous to that of the infant suffering from merycism in which the same food is swallowed, regurgitated, and re-swallowed again and again. In this process, the food is depleted of its nutritive value and eventually the infant may starve to death despite the fact that his mouth and stomach are regularly full.

I believe that both Fairbairn and Klein would be in full agreement with regard to what has been said thus far. One of Fairbairn's distinctive contributions to the analytic understanding of schizoid phenomena is his interpretation of the nature of schizoid anxiety. Whereas depressive anxiety is centered around the fear of the loss of the object as a result of one's destructive wishes toward the object, schizoid anxiety is based upon the fear that one's love is destructive to the object (Fairbairn, 1940). Since we are dealing with the earliest human relationship, that of mother and infant, the notion of the infant's love should be understood as virtually synonymous with the notion of the infant's way of being with and needing the mother. The dilemma is therefore a catastrophic one in that the infant feels that any sense of self that he has acquired, however rudimentary, is precisely that which will destroy the object upon whom he fully depends.[3]

With the background of this understanding of the schizoid condition, I shall focus on the most primitive sensation-dominated aspect of the schizoid personality, a dimension of experience barely touched upon in the work of either Klein or Fairbairn. I will propose that the schizoid condition can be thought of as Janus-faced: one face directed with fear and longing to the external object world that lies beyond the reach of the patient's illusions/delusions of omnipotence; the other face directed to a sensory-dominated state more primitive than that connected with the internal object world envisioned by Klein and Fairbairn. The latter "face" is the inarticulate underbelly of schizoid experience in which phantasy gives way to presymbolic, sensory-dominated experience.

The Contributions of Winnicott and Guntrip

At this point, I would like to briefly discuss portions of the work of Donald Winnicott and Harry Guntrip, who,

---

[3]Klein (1946, 1948, 1952b, 1955) understands schizoid anxiety as the outgrowth of inborn destructive impulses (derivatives of the death instinct) that undergo splitting and phantasied projection outward, thus creating a persecutory object world. Excessive splitting and evacuation of this sort pose a threat to the integrity of the ego, and are experienced in the form of a fear of impending annihilation. If fragmentation of the ego reaches a point where there is a breakdown of the paranoid-schizoid psychic organization, schizophrenic disorganization ensues.

along with Fairbairn and Klein, I view as the principal architects of the analytic understanding of schizoid phenomena. The discussion of Winnicott and Guntrip will center on their development of the beginnings of a conception of a sensory-based organization of experience more primitive than either Klein's conception of the paranoid-schizoid position or Fairbairn's notion of schizoid organization.

Winnicott

Winnicott's work shifted both the Kleinian and the Fairbairnian paradigms as they relate to a conception of early psychological organization and to schizoid phenomena. First, for Winnicott the unit of psychological development is not the infant, but an intersubjective entity, the mother–infant unit (Winnicott, 1952, 1956, 1971a). Secondly, Winnicott replaces the Kleinian and Fairbairnian conception of the splitting of the ego and object (followed by the elaboration of an internal object world) with a conception of a different sort of splitting of the personality. For Winnicott (1960b, 1963b), the split in the personality involves the alienation of a rudimentary experience of self (the True Self) from a compliant, externally-directed aspect of self (the False Self). The latter aspect of self is the Winnicottian equivalent of the schizoid aspect of personality.

Winnicott (1963b) states that in the beginning the space in which the infant lives is not an "internal" (p. 185) world in a Kleinian sense. Rather, " 'inner' only means personal and 'personal' is not yet individual" (1963b, p. 185). The True Self is a potential that has its origins in the earliest bodily sensations as experienced in the context of the relationship with the environmental mother: "The

True Self comes from the aliveness of the body tissues and the workings of the body functions, including the heart's action and breathing" (1960b, p. 148). The infant's world at this stage is not a world of external and internal object relations, but a world of "mere phenomena based on body experiences" (1963b, p. 183). Winnicott believes that even though the infant cannot alone sustain its own primitive psychological organization, such self-organization (which is primarily of a sensory sort) does exist because it is created by the mother–infant: "The True Self appears as soon as there is any mental organization of the individual at all, and it means little more than the summation of sensori-motor aliveness" (1960b, p. 149).

In this way, Winnicott points the way to a conception of an aspect of personality (more primitive than Klein's or Fairbairn's internal object world) in which there is a presymbolic, nondefensive isolation of the most rudimentary sense of self, which is centered in body experience. This early psychological organization fully depends upon the maternal provision of a facilitating environment. In the course of development by means of experience with transitional phenomena, the maternally-provided aspect of this state is taken over by the infant. (See Winnicott, 1951, and Ogden, 1986, for discussion of this process.)

Guntrip

Guntrip (1961, 1969) attempted an integration and extension of the work of Winnicott and Fairbairn. He proposed that in the course of the early development of every individual a portion of the unconscious ego (a split-off part of Fairbairn's [1944] "libidinal ego") undergoes regression to an insulated womb-like state. This regressed aspect of self remains a permanent part of the structure of the personality and exists in tension with more object-related aspects of self. Deeply regressed and insulated, this facet of the personality is far more extensive in the schizoid personality than in a more mature personality organization. "In this regressed state, the place of the good object is taken by the good environment, and there is a deep, obscure, but quite definite experience of feeling 'good and comfortable inside something' " (1961, p. 435). There is safety and potential for the emergence of the individuality of the self in the isolation of this regressed state; but there is also the danger of permanent loss of connectedness with both external and internal objects. Permanent disconnectedness from both the external and internal object world represents the threat of a terrifying loss of the self that is experienced as an impending suffocation. The internal object world is of critical importance as a defense against irreversible loss of the self in the regressed womb-like state. Thus, the schizoid organization of internal object relations is viewed by Guntrip as a middle ground between external object relations and a primitive object-less state.[4]

---

[4]Guntrip equates the regressed libidinal ego with the notion of a Winnicottian True Self "in cold storage till it can obtain a second chance to be reborn" (Guntrip, 1961, p. 432). I believe that this aspect of Guntrip's attempted integration of Fairbairnian and Winnicottian theory is the least satisfactory aspect of his work. It is based upon a mixing of metapsychologies that creates serious theoretical confusion. In Fairbairn's (1944) thinking, the libidinal ego is a split-off portion of the ego engaged in an unsatisfactory relationship with tantalizing objects. The attachment to the object is addictive in nature and interferes with the development of fulfilling whole object

I shall close this section by quoting at some length a statement by Michael Balint (1955). Balint captures with remarkable clarity and elegance the limits of the Fairbairnian and Kleinian conceptions of primitive experience and at the same time introduces a vital new way of describing the realm of early body experience alluded to in the work of Winnicott and Guntrip.

Practically all our technical terms describing the early period of mental life have been derived from objective phenomena and/or subjective experiences of the "oral" sphere; as for instance greed, incorporation, introjection, internalization, part-objects, destruction by sucking, chewing and biting, projection according to the pattern of spitting and vomiting, etc. Sadly enough, we have almost completely neglected to enrich our understanding of these very early, very primitive, phenomena by creating theoretical notions and coining technical terms using the experiences, imagery, and implications of other spheres. Such spheres are, among others, feelings of warmth, rhythmic noises and movements, subdued nondescript humming, the irresistible and overwhelming effects of tastes and smells, of close bodily contact, of tactile and muscle sensations especially in the hands, and the undeniable power of any and all of these for provoking and allaying anxieties and

---

relations and a genuine sense of self. Guntrip's "integration" therefore involves theoretical inconsistency in that it holds that the True Self (the core of one's individuality and sense of realness) has its origins in the libidinal ego, a portion of the personality engaged in a fundamentally pathological form of attachment to unattainable internal objects.

suspicions, blissful contentment and dire and desperate loneliness. [p. 241]

This chapter, and the previous two, represent a partial response to the "challenge" (p. 241) to psychoanalytic thinking posed by Balint (1955).

Clinical Illustration:
If a Tree Falls in the Forest

I shall now describe an aspect of the analysis of a patient, which has taught me a good deal about the relationship between schizoid internal object relations and an objectless, sensory-dominated world that forms its silent counterpart.

Ms. N., a 23-year-old graduate student, reluctantly began analysis because of intermittent bouts of crippling anxiety and a chronic feeling that she "failed to see the point in being alive."

The patient presented herself at the first meeting in a strikingly unadorned way. She wore a gray sweatshirt and jeans (which seemed identical to the clothing she would wear to every succeeding meeting for years); her hair was short, stringy, and unwashed. Ms. N. wore no make-up and later indicated that to do so would make her feel like a clown. Her manner was crisp, brusque, and sardonic. The patient never looked at me directly, although she occasionally stole a glance in my direction out of the corner of her eye when entering or leaving the office. During the first meeting, Ms. N. told me that the color of the walls of my office made the room feel to her like an ice cave.

In the initial months of analysis, Ms. N. was extremely guarded, repeatedly telling me how little she liked the idea of analysis, how absurd the whole set-up was, how little hope she had of getting anything out of it, and how completely alienated she felt from me. In this period there were frequent silences that, when allowed to continue, filled the entire meeting. These were tense silences that the patient said she experienced as "agonizing." Ms. N. said that she felt as if she were "drowning" in the futility of what we were "not doing."

It has been my experience that such silences can become a pernicious source of despair for schizoid patients, leading them to retreat into an increasingly withdrawn state. I entertained the hypothesis (in part on the basis of my countertransference experience of intense feelings of loneliness during the silences) that the silences in this case represented an enactment of pathological internal object relationships involving a mother and infant who each felt the other to be incapable of understanding the pain of the isolation of the other. On the basis of this hypothesis, I regularly talked to Ms. N. about what it was that I thought was going on between us, making it explicit that these were simply my ideas and that I could very well be quite wrong. My efforts were regularly met with the equivalent of the patient's rolling her eyes back in her head with disbelief about how stupid I could be. On occasion she would grudgingly admit to the possibility that there might be a grain of truth in what I said, but then would immediately ask what good that bit of wisdom did her.

At times this form of interaction had the familiar feel of work with an oppositional, but intact, adolescent patient. (It has been my experience that adolescent oppositionalism is usually a defense against loving and sexual feelings in the positive and negative Oedipal transferences.) However, this was not my predominant sense of what was going on in the analysis of Ms. N. The image of the ice cave mentioned by Ms. N. in the initial meeting echoed through me regularly during the initial years of this work. Just as I would feel the greatest need to encounter something living in the patient, I would be confronted by a form of self-sufficiency in her that was so unrelenting as to make me feel that I was dealing with a person who had not succeeded in becoming human.

Very gradually, over the first two years of the analysis, Ms. N. gave me small bits and pieces of information about herself. She did this almost parenthetically in an effort to deny the importance of a given memory or current incident in her life. Perhaps even more important to the patient was the need to disguise the fact that she had any desire whatever for me to know something about her. Ms. N.'s mother was described as "Normal with a capital N." She was an extremely "matter-of-fact" person who believed strongly that one can accomplish what one wants to and that any difficulty that one has in life is a form of self-indulgence. Almost entirely absent from her mother's vocabulary was any mention of feeling. The patient said that she had overheard her mother telling a friend that she had not breast-fed either of her children because it somehow seemed "unhygienic." One could boil the rubber nipples for plastic bottles, whereas in breast-feeding, there was no way to kill the germs.

Ms. N. described her father as a man who seemed as if he should have been somebody else's father. She said that he liked playing with his vintage sports cars, of which he had half a dozen. He spent almost all of his free time tinkering with them and "shining them up." The patient said that she had had the persistent fantasy as a child that neither of her parents was her real parent. She imagined that the people who claimed to be her parents were aliens who had secretly replaced her original parents and who knew how to act just like them. She would devise questions in her mind about minute details of past experiences with her real parents that only they would know about.

The patient had an older brother who felt to Ms. N. like "just another tenant in the boarding house." He seemed as if he knew how to go through all the right motions of getting good grades, doing well at sports, and so on, "but he just wasn't there and he didn't seem to know it." (The patient's descriptions of her family were like descriptions I have heard from other schizoid patients in that I could not keep a picture of the people being described in my mind for very long. For instance, I would often forget that the patient had a brother. The figures in the patient's life did not "come to life" in the patient's accounts, just as they had failed to come to life in her experience of them.)

Ms. N. was extremely secretive about the events of her current life. For instance, she took great pleasure in the fact that she had lived in a new apartment for over a year before I became aware of it through a hint that she dropped. It was a full two years before she told me that she was doing her doctoral studies in comparative literature.

The patient lived an extremely isolated and barren existence as a graduate student. She went to classes, had minimal contact with teachers and classmates, and spent most of her time in the various libraries of the university. There was a study cubicle in the stacks of the main library many floors below ground level (she never told me exactly how many) that was her "favorite place in the world." It had its own distinct smell of old, dusty books, its own particular coolness that never changed with the time of day or with the seasons, and its own peculiar lighting "that always seemed as if it were completely dark even though the lights were on."

I should emphasize that although what I learned from the patient is presented here in the form of a flowing narrative, this was not at all the style in which the information was conveyed to me by Ms. N. There was far more the feeling during those hours of painful pulling of teeth. The patient would haltingly give me a fragment of a story, apparently to see if I would pounce on it. If I displayed satisfactory restraint, I might be given another part of the story days or weeks later. If I were to ask a question, the patient would regularly fall silent for a period of five to ten minutes before giving me her highly crafted reply. Often she would not reply at all. I would occasionally inquire about what she was thinking and feeling during the periods of silence that followed my questions. Ms. N. would tell me that she was not thinking anything or that she was thinking about my question. It often seemed to me that despite my best efforts I had become engaged in a struggle of wills in which the first player to display any intensity of wishing for anything from the other was the loser. I was a novice playing against a grandmaster of the game.

I eventually said to Ms. N. that there was a good deal of her inability to talk to me that I thought was beyond her control. However, I suspected that there was a space, however small, in which she made conscious choices about that which she would tell me, how she would tell it to me, and when it would be told. I suggested that it would be useful to put into words what went into the choices that she made. I added that at times I suspected that she would experience it as a humiliating submission if she were to talk to me, and that she probably felt she would be flushing down the drain what little in her life she valued.

In response to these comments, Ms. N. said that when she was 4 or 5, or perhaps 6, she had overheard her aunt asking her mother a question that terrified her. Her aunt had asked her mother whether a tree that fell in the forest made any noise if no one were there to hear it. Ms. N. said that she had pictured herself alone in a forest yelling and not making any noise at all. This image had been so terrifying to her that she became afraid of going to sleep for fear of waking up alone in her room. I understood Ms. N.'s reply to my comments as her way of unconsciously explaining to me that each time she spoke to me there was the risk of her feeling as she had in that terrifying childhood image.

In the course of the third year of work with Ms. N., I gradually became aware of the intensity of a particular kind of strain that I experienced while with her. I found that I felt awkward, ill at ease, and self-conscious in a way that I rarely feel with patients with whom I have worked for very long. It was as if my ordinary way of conducting myself as an analyst was too rigid or unsuited to her in a way that I could not name. I often felt as if I were trying not to breathe while with her. As I became increasingly aware of this set of countertransference feelings and began to understand them in terms of projective identification, I said to Ms. N. that I thought that our being in the room together must feel to her like two people, each with a different communicable disease, who had been confined together in a small, unventilated room. (I was thinking of her mother's phantasy of the breast contaminating the baby and the baby contaminating the breast. In that phantasy the germs that constitute an ordinary part of the self were experienced as posing a danger to the other. I also was responding to my own fantasy of having to hold my breath while with this patient—perhaps this fantasy reflected my own unconscious fear of breathing out my own human germs or breathing in hers.)

As Ms. N. talked more about her secret place in the library, she began to refer to the fascination with words, language, and books that had played a major part in her life for as long as she could remember. She had spent endless hours as a child constructing elaborate fantasies that centered around plays on words, neologisms, puns, anagrams, rhymes, homonyms, and so on. She particularly liked a game that she had learned in school in which one invents a story with a moral that sounds like, or is the re-arrangement of, the words of an aphorism or a famous saying. She had read the dictionary for pleasure from the time that she was a 7-year-old, and incorporated abstruse words and the archaic use of words into her own thoughts.

As a child she would spend almost every afternoon in a local public library reading "shelf after shelf" of books. The subject matter was of no importance at all to her. She said that one would think that her knowledge would have become encyclopedic, but in fact she remembered almost nothing from what she read. She forgot the plots and facts as soon as she read them as if they had dropped into an enormous pit. She explained that there were many instances when she read the same book twice, realizing only at the very end of the book that she had previously read it. What would remind her of having read the book was not its contents, but some torn or missing page or some mark that she remembered on a page. The pleasure was in the "feeling of reading," which was in part a sound in her head, a soft, barely perceptible humming or buzzing, "like a fluorescent light bulb."

Again, in a casual manner that I was not supposed to pay much attention to, Ms. N. mentioned that as a 9-year-old she had discovered "treasure in the basement"—a trunk full of what she had assumed to be her father's collection of antique rifles and pistols along with some bullets and two old "Civil War-looking" swords. She said that the discovery had been extremely upsetting to her, but that she mentioned it to no one. It was as if her father's secret "arsenal" had made him a different person. She said that she remembers having looked at his face to see if she could discover this secret part of him in his eyes or facial expression.

In this period of the analysis (which at this point was in its fourth year), there was a gradually expanding feeling of calm that brought to mind the image of two enemy armies in a delicate truce during which each passing hour carried reason for hope, but also the question of how long the calm could possibly last and whether one might be operating under the influence of a dangerous illusion. The amount of time Ms. N. spent in the library stacks had diminished greatly by this point in the analysis. She had developed relationships with classmates and often studied in the main reading room with them. Her cubicle had become a place to which she could retreat as opposed to being the center of her life.

Several weeks after the patient's telling me about her discovery of the trunk in the basement, she came to one of our meetings in a state of extreme agitation. She began the hour by accusing me of secretly tape-recording our meetings. She felt furious at me, and deeply betrayed. I asked Ms. N. if she had any idea what it was that was frightening her. She said that she did not know, but that everything was frightening and that her mind was out of control. Over the weekend, she had not gone out of her apartment and had been terrified of letting anything in or out of it. She had unplugged her phone, her radio, and her television. Ms. N. said that she had not eaten or drunk anything except for bottled water because she was afraid of being poisoned. She was also terrified of urinating or defecating and imagined that if she were to do so, she would see blood and intestines in the toilet.

I said to her that there was nowhere inside or outside of her that she felt safe, and that the only thing she felt she could do was to try to keep what is outside out and what is inside in. Ms. N. said that that was right, and that she was so exhausted by the effort that she did not think that she could hold on much longer. She told me that her cubicle in the library was "losing its power." Over the previous weeks she had been aware of this change, but had not wanted to tell me because that would have made it more real.

The patient had begun to feel scared while in her library cubicle. For the first time she began to worry that somebody might lock the door leading to her floor and she might be trapped there. They might turn the lights out and she would starve to death without anyone knowing it. She could not rid herself of the horrible images she had of decaying there at her desk. She said that during all the years that she had gone to her cubicle, the thought had never once occurred to her that she might get locked in.

It seemed to me that Ms. N. was describing a number of different kinds of fears that were interconnected. I viewed the patient's experience in the library cubicle as one of being in a world dominated by autistic shapes—a self-soothing, almost completely insulated, asymbolic world of sensations in which there was hardly anything of a self. She existed there (or perhaps more accurately did not exist) out of time and place; she maintained a thin film of being by means of her reliance on the wholly predictable (mental) sound of reading, the smell of the books, the coolness of the air on her skin, and the physical sensation of the lighting, all of which never changed. It was a world removed from the ebb and flow (and unpredictability) of human relations.

Although this autistic-contiguous world had become an increasingly limited part of her life, Ms. N. felt utterly reliant on it as a place to which she could retreat. I said to her in the hour being described that I thought that she had felt for a long time that she was the ice cave that she had mentioned in our first meeting. It was not a matter of her living in an ice cave or living anywhere for that matter: she was the cave itself. There had at first been nothing inside of it or outside of it—there was just the cave. I went on to say that I thought that over the course of the previous years, there had begun to be life inside and outside of the cave. As a result, for the first time, for better or for worse, she could feel the fear of being trapped by herself; in the past few weeks in particular, it seemed that she had begun to feel that the cave was a place in which she could die and decay. Ms. N. then said that the idea of being trapped by herself in the stacks of the library was like being the tree falling in the forest where the noise that she makes does not make a sound.

It seemed to me that although they were extremely frightening, the delusions and persecutory anxiety that Ms. N. was currently experiencing took place in a world in which sounds could be heard. The patient had attempted to create a world of autistic isolation over the weekend in her apartment, but her attempts at securing safety in this way had failed. There was by now too much of a sense of self to allow her to flee into a world of pure sensation, unencumbered by external and internal objects. She was trapped in the world of objects. (I viewed the persecutory delusions as unconscious attempts at holding on to the world of internal objects in an effort to defend herself against autistic-contiguous anxiety, manifested in the fear of rotting, leaking, and having her insides fall out). Earlier in the analysis there had been no psychological context in which the patient could experience being alone in the cave because she *was* the inanimate cave. There had not yet been a sense of a living self that could be trapped and could rot, die, leak, and so on. In the period of analysis that followed the session being described, all of this was discussed with Ms. N. in much the same words that I have used here except for the use of the technical terms.

The succeeding year of analytic work had many of the features of a "contained psychosis." There was much blocking in the sessions, and the patient was preoccupied with a series of delusional ideas; however, she was able to keep this psychotic process from interfering with the relationships that she was developing with teachers, classmates, and the students with whom she was working as a teaching assistant in her department. This contained psychosis seemed to me to represent the patient's experiencing, in the analysis, the chronic psychosis that she had not been able to experience in childhood (cf. Winnicott, 1974). The childhood psychosis had been foreclosed through the use of defensive withdrawal into a world of autistic shapes (e.g., the "sound" of reading). This period of the work was a phase of "reworking" of the patient's autistic-contiguous anxiety, in a predominantly paranoid-schizoid context of part-object relations, symbolic equation, splitting, omnipotent thinking, projective identification, and persecutory anxiety.

The following dream of Ms. N.'s is an example of the way in which the patient unconsciously attempted to grapple with her fears of rotting (a manifestation of anxiety of an autistic-contiguous type) in a more symbolically grounded, object-related psychological context:

There was a ferocious storm. The walls and ceilings of Ms. N.'s apartment were covered with water that was seeping through from the outside. The patient discovered with horror that a book she valued more than anything in the world was swollen with water. As she picked up the book to see if she could dry it out, the binding came apart in clumps in her hands. She woke up in a state of panic.

The patient was able to talk about this dream in terms of fears (with which she was by this time familiar) of her insides rotting and her skin decaying. She was also able to understand that for years she had felt that this disaster was actually occurring during her menstrual periods. (Her periods, which had ceased when she was 19, had resumed about six months prior to her reporting this dream.) Ms. N. said that for the first time in her life she could feel her stomach inside of her. In the past, she had been unable to feel anything in her abdomen where she knew her stomach should be. She guessed that that was why she could not be sure that it would stay where it was supposed to.

In this reworking, there was a complicated interplay of all three modes of experience including the depressive mode. (The latter was reflected in part in the patient's capacity to observe and interpret both her waking and dreaming experience.) An important shift in the interplay of modes of experience had taken place. While in the initial years of analysis there was strong evidence of experience being generated both in autistic-contiguous and in paranoid-schizoid modes, each mode served to isolate the patient not only from communication with external objects, but also from a conscious and unconscious internal dialogue. The reworking involved in the patient's contained psychosis reflected the transformation of pathologically hypertrophied autistic-contiguous defenses (designed to prevent the development of the experience of self, and the formation of symbols with which to communicate that experience), into a form of autistic-contiguous experience which increasingly came to serve as a sensory foundation for the patient's sense of self. The latter is presymbolic (as opposed to asymbolic) and allowed the patient to generate the beginnings of a dialectical interplay between sensory-dominated experience of self, and forms of the experience of self that were more grounded in symbols and in relationships with external and internal objects (i.e., experience in paranoid-schizoid and depressive modes).

As this work progressed, Ms. N. told me — with intense feelings of guilt and a conviction that I would hate her — that she had lied to me. She said that she had not simply "happened upon" the trunk in the basement of her parents' home. It had been necessary to "rummage through" the keys in her father's dresser drawer, which was clearly part of his "private stuff," in order to find the key that she was looking for. Moreover, after discovering the contents of the trunk, she had not, as she had told me, fearfully stayed away from it. In fact, over a period of years, she had made regular "visits" to the trunk in order to examine and handle its contents. She had not simply been horrified by her father's secret, she had felt excited by it and imagined that she, and she alone, had discovered his "boyish soul." She had cherished the idea that he must have been very much like her, in having these secrets. Ms. N. had felt that he too must have had his own private inner world. As she returned to this topic in subsequent meetings, she added that the trunk had been a source of sexual excitement for her and that the sensations and images connected with the rifles, swords, and bullets had been a regular part of her masturbatory fantasies.

Ms. N. said that she now felt that her intrusion into her father's privacy was the equivalent of an "act of rape." She told me that she often experienced me as an innocent, like her father. I seemed to her to be completely unaware of the way in which she used all of her deviousness to get inside of me, as she now felt that she literally got inside of her father. (I heard in this a reference to the patient's sexual interest in me and her wish that I find her sexually exciting. These wishes were in part expressed in changes in her way of carrying herself and in the style of the clothes that she wore.) The patient said that she had never succeeded in getting inside of her mother. It was as if she could "never find an inside to get inside of." The patient said that she felt as sorry for her mother as she did for herself when she described her mother in this way.

This led to the patient's talking about how lonely it must have been for me to have been so coldly treated by her for so long. She said that for years she had experienced me as trying to pry her open while remaining perfectly opaque myself, but she now felt that it was she who had been trying to get inside of me while remaining as impenetrable as the monolith in the film *2001*. (The sexual meaning of the idea of getting inside of another person was not directly addressed at this point, but later became a central focus of the analytic work.)

In a meeting that followed some weeks later, Ms. N. upon entering my office handed me a worn paperback copy of Faulkner's *The Sound and the Fury*. She said that, as I well knew, she hated "sentimental slop," but that she wanted to give me this book. I thanked her and put it on the table beside me. She told me to "read the damn thing and see if you can learn anything from it." She added that she was certain I had already read it, but that I should read it again. (Ms. N. was not going to risk having me tell her that I had already read the book. In fact, I had never read the book that she gave me because the book that I was to read was most importantly *her book*.) With that she turned over on the couch to face the wall, clearly indicating that I should begin reading it right there and then. For the next few meetings, I read. I felt under no pressure to do anything but read. It was not difficult to understand why this was a book much cherished by Ms. N. I could feel more powerfully than I had in previous readings that this book was a sacred rendering of a man's most private self. It had to be read as I imagined the patient would like to be listened to—with a state of mind that allows words to wash over the reader without the need for explanation and with tremendous tolerance for confusion. This kind of receptivity (what Bion [1962] would call "reverie") is the antithesis of the tree falling in the forest. The book reminded me of the patient: there was something wispy and romantic about it (while all the time denying its romanticism). At the same time, there was something tough, uncompromising, and unforgiving about the language. Faulkner allows the reader to know only so much and no more—there is a core that one can glimpse fleetingly through one's senses, not through one's intellect.

After a few meetings, the patient said that I could finish reading the book on my own if I wanted to. She said that she had liked spending the previous few sessions as we had, but that now there were things that she wanted to talk about. Over the course of the following months, Ms. N. periodically returned to talking about those meetings. The patient said that she had felt close to me while I was reading. She told me that during most of the time that I was reading she had not been thinking. Instead she had had the sense that there was a "hub" in the middle of the room between us. It was as if there had been a kind of gravity that had held us to it and a kind of centrifugal force that had kept us from bumping into one another.

In this part of the analysis, there was further re-working of autistic-contiguous experience, this time in a predominantly depressive mode. The patient's earlier feelings of having been the victim both of her parents' coldness and of my "analytic intrusiveness" were now experienced in a new psychological context. The patient recognized and took responsibility for her own coldness, her own fantasied and actual acts of plundering the privacy of others. Ms. N. seemed able to begin to tolerate her own wishes for sexual aliveness both in the present and in the past. Her sexual and romantic love for me in the paternal transference was evident to both of us, although not yet directly put into words. There was the capacity for empathy for me, and even the beginnings of compassion for her mother's seemingly complete inability to generate her own internal life.

The gift of the book was an important act of reparation. Not to have accepted it would have repre-

sented a countertransference acting-out of an unconscious identification with an internal object incapable of
tolerating, recognizing, and accepting the affection and
reparative wishes of the other. The gift was an expression
of the patient's love that was only perfunctorily disguised;
at the same time it seemed to represent a plea that I not
try to find out all about her: I should understand that
there are some things that must not be understood too
well.

Summary

Despite the enormous clinical and theoretical importance
of the concepts associated with Fairbairn's conception of
the internal object world, and Klein's notion of the
paranoid-schizoid position, these ideas have not been
sufficient to provide a full understanding of schizoid
phenomena. In this chapter, I have attempted to demonstrate that analytic work with schizoid patients must be
informed by an understanding of the way in which
schizoid phenomena represent a realm of experience that
lies between a world of timeless, strangulated internal
object relations and a more primitive, inarticulate, sensory-
based world of autistic shapes and objects.

5

The Transitional Oedipal Relationship in Female Development

Transitions from one psychological organization to another are of particular importance in psychoanalytic thinking and yet are among the most difficult aspects of psychological development to conceptualize. The present chapter attempts to make a contribution to the psychoanalytic understanding of the transition in female development that occurs at the threshold of the Oedipus complex.

The early phase of the female Oedipus complex will be viewed as a pivotal moment in development in which a form of transitional relationship to the mother mediates the little girl's entry into Oedipal object love. This transitional relationship is similar to, but distinct from, the earlier relationship to the transitional object described by Winnicott (1951, 1971a). The paradoxical nature of the little girl's transitional Oedipal relationship (created by mother and daughter) lies in the fact that the first triadic object relationship occurs in the context of a two-person relationship; the first heterosexual relationship develops in a relationship between two females; the father as libidinal object is discovered in the mother.

From the perspective of this understanding of the little girl's entry into the Oedipus complex, there will be a reexamination of Freud's conception of the role of castration fantasies and penis envy in the female Oedipal narrative. Forms of character pathology deriving from inadequacy of this transitional Oedipal relationship will be described. Finally, a form of transference–countertransference difficulty encountered in the treatment of female patients will be understood as reflecting problems arising from the period of early Oedipal development that is under discussion.

The Female Oedipal Narrative

Redirection of the little girl's libidinal attachment from her mother to her father in the positive Oedipus complex is a development step that has not been adequately understood. Many analysts have understood this movement as a reflection of innate heterosexuality (Chasseguet-Smirgel, 1964; Horney, 1926; Jones, 1935; Klein, 1928; Parens et al., 1976; Stoller, 1973).

Freud (1933) rejected the notion of a biological explanation[1] for the shift in libidinal attachment in

---

[1]Freud is somewhat self-contradictory here since the Oedipus complex is a structural concept positing a universal biologically determined organization of wishes and meanings (see Ogden, 1984). The positive Oedipus complex by definition includes genital-level sexual wishes toward the parent of the opposite sex, and therefore involves inherent, biologically determined heterosexual strivings. The negative Oedipus complex similarly posits (universal) inherent strivings toward a homosexual love relationship with the parent of the same sex.

female Oedipal development, and insisted that the movement toward the father be understood in psychological terms. Freud (1925, 1931, 1933) viewed castration anxiety and shame in connection with the lack of a penis as the major forces in the little girl's turn from the mother to the father.

> At the end of this first [pre-Oedipal] phase of attachment to the mother, there emerges, as the girl's strongest motive for turning away from her, the reproach that her mother did not give her a proper penis — that is to say, brought her into the world as a female. [1931, p. 234]

> The turning away from the mother is accompanied by hostility; the attachment to the [pre-Oedipal] mother ends in hate. [1933, pp. 121–122]

> . . . [we] learn from analyses that girls hold their mother responsible for their lack of a penis and do not forgive her for their being thus put at a disadvantage. [1933, p. 124]

In this rendering of the female Oedipus narrative, the little girl is ashamed and disappointed by her discovery that she lacks a penis. She also feels contempt for her "castrated" mother (Freud, 1933). As a result, she turns away in anger and disappointment from the mother. In the mind of the child, according to Freud, the mother's refusal to provide the little girl with a penis reflects the mother's lack of love for her daughter. Therefore, in her feelings of deficiency and shame (as well as contempt), the little girl angrily turns to her father as her replacement love object. She hopes that her father's love (and more concretely, her father's baby) will make up for her lack of a penis.

> Not until the emergence of the wish for a penis [in the Oedipus complex] does the doll-baby become a baby from the girl's father, and thereafter the aim of the most powerful feminine wish. Her happiness is great if later on this wish for a baby finds fulfillment in reality, quite especially so if the baby is a little boy who brings the longed-for penis with him. [1933, p. 128]

I believe that there are significant theoretical difficulties posed by Freud's female Oedipal narrative. First of all, there is inadequate differentiation between pre-Oedipal and Oedipal object relations. The girl is seen as "shifting" her object cathexis from the mother to the father. What is glossed over in this formulation of the "shift" is that the status of the mother as "object" and the status of the father as "object" are not at all equivalent. The transition is not from one object to another, but from a relationship to an internal object (an object that is not completely separate from oneself) to a cathexis of an external object (an object that exists outside of one's omnipotence). The external object encountered is not only the Oedipal father, but also the Oedipal mother with whom the Oedipal father has a relationship. (This relationship between the external mother and the external father is at the core of what generates the triangulation that to a large extent defines the Oedipus complex.)

The pre-Oedipal mother is an object that partakes of the child's omnipotence. Abrupt disillusionment in the pre-Oedipal period leads not to an advance to whole-object relatedness, but to a redoubling of the child's efforts at omnipotent defensive solutions worked out in relation to internal objects. (See Schafer, 1974, for a critique of Freud's "shock theory" of the female entry into the Oedipus complex.) It is only a healthy, well-dosed disillusionment process that results in a movement from omnipotent object relations to an investment in external objects that lie outside one's control. A movement to a cathexis of both the Oedipal mother and father is a developmental advance to an involvement with external objects, and therefore requires a healthy weaning experience mediated by transitional objects and phenomena (Winnicott, 1951; see also Ogden, 1985a). Disruption of the pre-Oedipal relationship with the mother in the manner described by Freud would be expected to lead to the erection of narcissistic defenses and object relatedness, schizoid withdrawal from external objects, and/or a reintensification of reliance on omnipotent defenses. These forms of defense allow the child the illusion of absolute control over his or her object world (the world of internal objects).

Secondly, Oedipal love is the foundation of healthy whole-object love relations. Shame and a sense of failure and defectiveness are not the ingredients that propel one into a healthy love relationship. A love relationship entered into as a result of a flight from shame and narcissistic injury is almost certain to be constructed for the purpose of narcissistic defense, and is unlikely to involve genuine object love. It is only a foundation of healthy narcissism, generating feelings of hope and of openness to the unknown, that prepares the way for the little girl's taking the risk of falling in love with the external-object father—a person outside of her omnipotent control. The picture of the little girl shamefully, defeatedly, and angrily turning away from the mother to

the father is at odds with one of the most fundamental
psychoanalytic propositions: the concept of the Oedipus
complex as the cornerstone of the development of mature
object love.

   Thirdly, the Freudian narrative of the female Oedipus complex rests upon the assumption that the little
girl's discovery that she lacks a penis is, for her, a
profoundly disappointing event that constitutes a turning
point in development. Few analysts would dispute the
idea that penis envy is encountered in the analysis of
every female (and every male) patient. That castration
fantasies and penis envy exist in little girls is not the issue.
The question is whether it is the little girl's anger at her
mother for not giving her a penis that is the "strongest
motive" (Freud, 1931) leading the little girl to reject the
mother and turn to her father as the object of libidinal
desire. Observational studies of Parens and colleagues
(1976) have shown that castration anxiety does not
consistently precede the appearance of the little girl's
entry into the Oedipus complex as reflected by a "seemingly heterosexual attitude toward her father" (p. 85), her
wish to have a baby, and her rivalry with her mother.
There is a question of whether castration anxiety in girls
primarily involves the phantasy of the loss of a once-
possessed penis, or whether female castration anxiety
primarily involves phantasies of damage to the female
genitals (Applegarth, 1985). There is a further question
of whether the little girl predominantly experiences her
own genitals as reflecting the result of the loss of the
penis; or whether, in normal development, she predominantly perceives the female genitals to be the standard of
normalcy, believing that little boys possess defective
equipment that is "too closed" and "unreceptive" to work
well (Mayer, 1985).

A narrative of the female Oedipus complex must account for the little girl's turning from the mother to the father in the course of this phase of development. I believe that the Freudian narrative must be reformulated in the light of enhanced psychoanalytic understandings of early object relations, and of the psychological-interpersonal processes mediating the nontraumatic movement from internal to external object relations.

The Developmental Context

Before presenting my understanding of the transitional relationship with the mother that mediates the entry into the female Oedipus complex, I would like to briefly review some of the features of psychological development forming the context for this moment in development.

Psychological development involves the elaboration of an increasing capacity for awareness of otherness, mediated by interpersonal processes and the maturation of the infant's biological and psychological capacities. Although there is progressive movement throughout development toward the "discovery of externality" (Winnicott, 1968), there are critical periods of psychological reorganization in which new capacities for object relatedness are developed that are qualitatively different from pre-existing forms of relatedness (cf. Spitz, 1965).

Early infantile experience involves the coexistence of two aspects of relatedness to the mother. One aspect of the mother–infant relationship involves the relationship to the environmental mother (the mother as holding environment); the other involves the relationship to the mother as object (Winnicott, 1963b). In the beginning, the former aspect of relatedness far outweighs the latter.

The balance shifts in the course of development until the relationship to the mother as environment becomes the silent background of object-related experience (variously referred to as the "background object of primary identification" [Grotstein, 1981], the "dream screen" [Lewin, 1950], and the "matrix of the mind" [Ogden, 1985a, 1986]).

In the relationship to the environmental mother, experience is generated in a predominantly homogeneous field: there is very little experience of difference, for example, the difference between inside and outside, me and not-me, presentation and re-presentation. This psychological state is mediated by the mother's provision of the illusion of the "subjective object" (Winnicott, 1962, 1967a), wherein the mother meets the infant's need so unobtrusively that she is hardly noticed. The subjective object is experienced as if it had been "created" (Winnicott, 1951) by the infant according to his needs. And yet the idea of the infant "creating the object" is misleading since the infant has little sense of himself as a separate entity, much less the creator of people and things.

The question arises as to how it is possible for the infant to move nontraumatically from the protective illusion of the subjective object to a capacity to experience objects as independent of himself. The infant's discovery of an external reality (which long preceded him) must be mediated interpersonally. Winnicott (1951) has described this process (which begins at "about four to six to eight to twelve months" [p. 4]) as one in which a psychological state based upon a series of paradoxes is generated and maintained by mother and infant. The state of mind created in this way underlies the child's relationship to a transitional object. The transitional object is an object that is both discovered and created; it is both reality and fantasy; both me and not-me; both the omnipotent, protective, internal object *mother,* and the external object *thing* with its own fixed sensory qualities. Most importantly, the question of which it is — created or discovered, me or not-me — never arises.

Winnicott's concept of the discovery of externality mediated by a relationship to the transitional object, is a conception of development that differs from a view of development as advancing from union to separateness through a gradual process of well-dosed frustration that is in step with the child's maturing ego capacities. The relationship to a transitional object is not a halfway point in a weaning process through which awareness of separateness develops linearly in small increments. As I have discussed elsewhere (Ogden, 1985a,b), transitional phenomena have a dialectical structure. Oneness and separateness, reality and fantasy, me and not-me coexist with one another, each creating, preserving, and negating the other. Reality does not supersede fantasy any more than the conscious mind replaces the unconscious mind in the course of development. Rather, reality enters into a mutually defining and enriching relationship with fantasy. It is only in the space between reality and fantasy created in this way that subjectivity, personal meaning, symbol formation, and imagination become possible.

As mentioned above, the discovery of externality is an ongoing process from birth, and yet there are critical periods of reorganization from which the capacity for qualitatively new modes of object relatedness emerge. The entry into the Oedipus complex represents one such pivotal period of development. The entry into the Oedipus complex involves the introduction of a distinctly new form of otherness into the mother–infant dyad that requires a radical psychological-interpersonal reorganization.

The Transitional Relationship

The psychological reorganization involved in the entry into the female Oedipus complex is mediated by a particular form of transitional relationship to the mother. As with the earlier forms of transitional phenomena, the function of this relationship is the introduction of otherness in a form that is at first experienced as other and not-other at the same time. In a state of mind in which such a paradox can be created and maintained by mother and child, a manageable transition is set in motion that will obviate the child's need to construct a rigid defensive system to protect the self from intolerable (premature) awareness of separateness. In the case of the Oedipal situation, the father is the principal representative of otherness.[2] In addition, the mother of the Oedipus complex is a far more external object than she had been previously, although the relationship to the Oedipal mother never loses its connection with the experience of the mother as subjective object (cf. Chodorow, 1978). The discovery of the Oedipal mother's externality is

---

[2]Lacan (1956–1957) has pointed out that it is not the power of the individual personality of the father that is of central importance in liberating the infant from the "realm of the imaginary," in which the infant is imprisoned in a nonsubjective world of immediate lived sensory experience. Rather, the father's power lies in his role as the carrier of symbols, as representative of a system of meanings (organized in language) that provides the child with the means by which to mediate between himself and his sensory experience.

always experienced, in part, as a betrayal. The child says, in effect, "I thought that we had an agreement that what's yours is mine and what's mine is yours, so why do I have to knock on the door of your bedroom [that you share with father] before going in? I didn't have to before." The anger connected with this is directed more at the mother than at the father, since, in the little girl's mind, it is the mother who is "defecting," "changing the rules."

The psychological reorganization required at the threshold of the female Oedipus complex is extensive. Both mother and father are discovered (to a much fuller degree than before) as external objects. The child becomes aware of her parents as people who have an intimate relationship with one another that does not include her. At the same time, an intense, triangulated set of whole-object relationships is established in which the father is taken as love object, while the mother is established as an ambivalently loved rival. This reorganization takes place nontraumatically because it is mediated by a relationship with the mother that embodies the following paradox: *the little girl falls in love with the mother-as-father and with the father-as-mother*. From a psychoanalytic perspective, what occurs in this transitional relationship is that the little girl falls in love with the (not yet fully external) mother who is engaged in an unconscious identification with her own father in her internal set of Oedipal object relations. The question of whether the little girl is in love with her mother or her father (in love with an internal object or an external object) never arises. It is both. She is in love with her mother-as-father and her father-as-mother. This paradox is the core of what allows the entry into the Oedipus complex to be achieved without overwhelming disillusionment that would require growth-limiting defensive maneuvers. The little girl does not have to reject the mother in order to love the father; she does not have to renounce an internal object for an external object.

The role of the mother as Oedipal transitional object is to allow herself to be loved as a man (her own unconscious identification with her own father). In so doing, she unconsciously says to her daughter, "If I were a man, I would be in love with you, find you beautiful, and would very much want to marry you." Since the unconscious mind knows nothing of "If I were. . . ," the mother's unconscious communication is more accurately stated as "I am a man, your father, and am in love with you, find you beautiful, and want to marry you."

The mother in this relationship allows herself to be used as a conduit to a relationship with "the other," who paradoxically is already a part of herself in her own identification with the other (her own father). Green (1975), expanding upon Winnicott's (1960a) idea that there is no such thing as an infant, has said that there is no such thing as a mother and infant, since the father is always represented in the unconscious mind of the mother. This idea has particular significance at the moment in development that is being described. The mother's capacity to serve in the transitional role under discussion is compromised to the degree to which her unconscious relationship with her own Oedipal father is conflicted.

To summarize, the entrance into the female Oedipus complex does not initially revolve around a relationship with the father himself, but around the mother's unconscious identification with her own father (more accurately, the mother's internal object relationship with her own father). The early period of female Oedipal development involves a triangulation of object relations achieved in the context of a two-person relationship. Before the little girl is capable of a relationship with the other (the father), she and her mother engage in a "dress rehearsal" for the later Oedipal drama in which the actual father (a much more fully external object than the mother-as-father) will become central. The metaphor of the dress rehearsal conveys something of the way in which the transitional Oedipal relationship with the mother is a form of play that is a real experience in its own right, and yet is preparatory for something else that is felt to be "more real." The dress rehearsal is conducted in the safety of the privacy of the dyad, and yet the other — the father — is very much present (in imagination).

In latency and adolescence, the Oedipal transitional relationship between mother and daughter is reenacted in a wide variety of forms. One of the common forms of this reenactment is the "shopping expedition" during which the daughter tries on clothes while the mother participates through an identification with the man (unconsciously an identification with the mother's own father in relation to herself as a little girl). The mother (as a man) admires her daughter. The girl's father is physically absent at the moment, but is very much the emotionally present third party in this drama. It is to a large degree the father that the little girl sees in the mother's gaze.

The aspect of the mother–daughter relationship that I am focusing on is different from the mother's vicarious enjoyment of her daughter's pleasure in her (the daughter's) Oedipal romance with the father. The latter is undoubtedly an important element in a later phase of Oedipal development, and involves a revival of the pleasure the mother experienced in her Oedipal experience with her own father. However, this aspect of experience involves the actual involvement of the little girl's father, and therefore is developmentally later than the aspect of development I am focusing on.

The transitional Oedipal relationship must also be distinguished from the female negative Oedipus complex wherein the mother is taken as a romantic and sexual object while the father is seen as the rival. In the form of relatedness that I am describing, the mother both is the father and is not the father; the question of whether she is mother *or* father is never asked. In contrast, the love of the mother in the negative Oedipus complex is a genital-level romantic and sexual attachment of one female for another. For the little girl, the ambivalently loved father is an unwelcome interference whom she wishes to get rid of. This is clearly quite different from the situation involved in the transition into the positive Oedipus complex.

It is the success of the early Oedipal transitional relationship that paves the way for the little girl's act of courage in allowing herself to fall in love with the actual father. Her father, after all, is a person who lies beyond the realm of the little girl's omnipotence, and she must take her chances with him. It is possible that he will not reciprocate her love, thus disappointing and/or humiliating her. If this should occur, she inevitably draws the conclusion that there must be something the matter with her that would cause her father to find her unlovable. Since it is romantic and sexual feelings, in addition to wishes to displace her mother, that are most intense in the Oedipal period, it is these aspects of herself that are usually thought to be the basis of her unacceptability.[3]

---

[3]These Oedipal-level feelings are much more circumscribed and nameable than are the earlier feelings of incompleteness or failure

Psychopathology and the Oedipal Transitional Relationship

The Oedipal transitional relationship to the mother is a form of relatedness through which the mother unconsciously gives her blessing to the little girl's Oedipal love of her father, and, from there, her love of other men. Inadequacy of this transitional relationship stifles (in phantasy, involves a prohibition of) the development of the little girl's interest in the father. It becomes necessary for the little girl to deny wishes and strivings in relation to the father, and to deny the thought that the father has anything to offer her. If the father does not attempt to override the mother's unconscious prohibition of the Oedipal romance, the little girl feels confirmed in her belief that she should not have romantic and sexual feelings for her father (and rivalrous feelings for her mother) and that the feelings she does have are bad — too disloyal, too dirty, too intense, too greedy, directed at the wrong person, and so on. Whether or not the father is emotionally available to the little girl in this stage of development, the mother's inability or unwillingness to serve as an Oedipal transitional object is interpreted (often correctly so) as an unwillingness on the part of the mother to condone the little girl's entry into Oedipal object relations. Such a mother is unable to identify with

---

that result from a mother's inability to recognize and accept the infant's love. The earliest experience of a "lack of fit" between mother and infant leads the infant to feel that it is his or her way of loving that is hurtful (Fairbairn, 1940). This represents the most global and fundamental damnation of self. It is one's way of being with the other, and not simply one's hostility or sexual feelings, that are unacceptable.

her own father in a way that serves a transitional function. To enter into an Oedipal relationship with the father under these circumstances involves a dangerous attempt to bypass the mother. This is an extremely difficult task in the absence of the father's active assistance. Even the wish to be like the father is experienced as a forbidden act and as a betrayal of the mother. This identification with the father is unconsciously experienced by the little girl as an attempt to *be* what she cannot, and should not, *have*. It is felt to be an act of stealing what she senses should not be hers. This fear of identification with the Oedipal father frequently manifests itself in adulthood as a "hyper-feminine" stance wherein the woman acts as if she cannot do anything or have any knowledge of anything "masculine"—for example, being able to engage in logical, scientific thought and discussion, being able to select a car, and doing basic home repairs.

Another form of character defense that often originates as a result of pathology in the transitional Oedipal relationship is the pervasive feeling that "there is nothing a man can do that I can't and therefore no man has anything to offer me." This represents an outgrowth of the unconscious conviction that love of the Oedipal father is a betrayal of the mother. One such analysand, employed as a social worker, consistently put herself in dangerous situations in relation to violent male patients in order to unconsciously demonstrate that there was nothing a man could do that she could not. She did not need anybody's help, particularly the assistance of the male members of the staff. There was utter denial of the fact that most men were larger and stronger than she. Such an acknowledgment would have been profoundly humiliating for her, since it was unconsciously equivalent to an acknowledgment of her wish that her father would offer her something she valued and could not provide for herself. In the extreme, this leads to a pathological form of homosexual object choice.[4]

I would now like to offer a brief clinical example illustrating transference experiences of transitional Oedipal object relatedness.

The patient, L., was a 27-year-old graduate student at the time she came to therapy expressing feelings of extreme loneliness and pointlessness. She dressed in a rather masculine way, with severe-looking short hair. The therapist experienced herself when with this patient as a caricature of femininity alternating between the sweet, prissy little girl and the earth mother with enormous, disgusting, suffocating breasts. (This was understood as a reflection of the patient's use of splitting and projective identification.) L. felt strongly that men are ruthless, power-hungry, and without feelings, while women are weak, ineffectual, and pathetic.

The patient derived no pleasure from sex either with men or with women and had given up sex altogether five years earlier. She occasionally attempted to masturbate, but was unable to achieve orgasm. During masturbation, she "unaccountably" found tears rolling down her cheeks. She reported experiencing the faintest glimmer of the feelings of sadness and futility, but there was no conscious sexual fantasy or imagery connected with the tears.

---

[4]I concur with McDougall's (1986) conception that "the variations in psychosexual structure are so great that we are obliged to talk in the plural: of heterosexualities and homosexualities" (p. 20). A particular form of sexuality, whether heterosexual or homosexual, is considered pathological to the degree that it serves to circumvent the individual's entry into or "elaboration of . . . the depressive position" (p. 23).

L.'s father had abandoned her mother before the patient was born. The patient's mother had then buried herself in her work and had a series of relationships with men whom she never introduced or even mentioned to the patient. L.'s mother refused to tell her anything about her father.

It is not possible here to trace the development of this intensive therapy to the point in the sixth year of work that will be focused upon, other than to say that the schizoid withdrawal and splitting defenses gradually diminished, giving way to the beginnings of ambivalence and whole-object relatedness.

Over a period of months in the sixth year of therapy, L. would stare at the therapist, saying at first that she saw something in her eyes but did not know what it was. Over time she said she also heard this same thing in the therapist's voice. It was unfamiliar, but fascinating—it was a "hardness that wasn't harsh or cold." The patient said, after weeks of circumlocutions, that there was something "sexy" about it, but added that it was terribly important that the therapist not misunderstand this as homosexual. It was not at all what she had felt for women whom she had felt attracted to and at times felt she was in love with. On the other hand, it was a bodily experience that she had not had in years and never expected to have again.

At that point in the therapy, the patient became interested in a "purely intellectual way" in a male professor several years older than she. L. felt very self-conscious talking to the therapist about this man, but eventually was able to haltingly talk about how the man lived in "an entirely different world" from her, a world in which she felt unable to speak the language or know the customs. As a result she alternately felt either invisible or as if she were a freak. She was extremely anxious that both the professor and the therapist might see her as a fool for being interested in a man who would obviously have no interest in her. In addition, she became angry and somewhat paranoid about the fact that the therapist also lived so comfortably in that different world and would have no interest in helping the patient become a part of it, and in fact might actively attempt to exclude the patient from it. In her therapy, the link between these feelings and L.'s experience of her mother was interpreted. At the same time the patient also felt that to enter that world would be a betrayal of her feminist and lesbian friends, and that a bungled attempt at entering that world would leave her absolutely alone, unable and undeserving to turn in either direction.

In a state of panic, L. withdrew from the relationship with the professor and refocused her attention on the "soft, feminine hardness that wasn't coldness" that she saw and heard in the therapist. L. confessed with great embarrassment that she was very taken with this quality of the therapist; she said, however, "I'm not in love with you, but with that feeling I brush up against in experiencing that part of you I've been trying to describe. To fall in love with you would be like being trapped in a dark, musty cave and I have no desire for that again [something she had experienced in a brief homosexual affair]. To fall in love with you in that way would be to step onto wet grass and find you're sinking up to your knees, instead of sinking for a moment until the firmness of the ground holds you."

The patient in this period said that she was feeling curious about her father for the first time since childhood. She had looked at pictures taken of herself from her childhood to the present (an activity she had been phobic about to this point) in order to see if she could figure out what her father looked like by "subtracting" the features she knew to be her mother's. She had made a conscious effort as a child not to look for her father in the men she saw on the street. The therapist suggested that the patient was feeling that there are men to be found in women and women to be found in men, and that perhaps this was the meaning of the patient's discovery of the hardness that wasn't coldness in the therapist.

Several months later, L. wore a skirt and blouse to her therapy session for the first time. She was clearly anxious, walked into the office with her head down, her eyes fixed on her shoes. When she finally looked up at the therapist, they both smiled. The patient's eyes filled with tears. She said that the therapist's smile had been one of the warmest and most quietly accepting moments of her life. (The therapist had to stifle her own tears because the patient appeared to her to be placing herself in the therapist's hands so innocently and trustingly that she was reminded of experiences with both her own children and her own mother.) L. said that she had been so afraid that the therapist would laugh at her that she had changed her clothes six times before finally mustering the courage to wear the skirt and blouse to the session.

The material at this point became centered on the patient's fantasies of the therapist's relationship with her husband, at first with the patient as the fantasied child. Later, with considerable anxiety, the patient reported a dream in which the therapist's husband asked his wife who that woman [the patient] was whom he had seen leaving the therapist's office. L. began to be able to entertain conscious sexual fantasies (including during masturbation) which centered on a "torrid affair" between herself (identified with Lauren Bacall, "a gutsy woman") and Humphrey Bogart.

The patient in this sequence of events had initially utilized schizoid withdrawal and splitting defenses (including the splitting of masculinity and femininity) to ward off the dangers and complexity of Oedipal relatedness. Once having achieved the beginnings of the capacity for whole-object relatedness in the depressive position, she developed the potential for more than fleeting and scattered elements of Oedipal relatedness. This was ushered in by the patient's seeing and hearing in the therapist a hardness-in-softness, the father-in-mother, maleness-in-femaleness. It was not the mother in a negative Oedipal transference that was the predominant issue here; rather, it was the transitional role of the discovery of a heretofore frightening otherness in the familiar. It was essential that the familiar not be too familiar—that is, not too much the mother of the primitive mother–infant dyad (the dark, musty cave and the wet ground that swallows one up). It was equally important that the "other," the unfamiliar, not be too frighteningly alien and unwelcoming (the "other world" the professor lived in). The patient's experience was of falling in love with the transference mother who was not entirely the mother ("It's not you I'm in love with"); and of falling in love with the father (in the mother), the hardness in the softness, that was not yet the father as fully external object. This was a critical transferential experience (that was interpreted), leading to the patient's daring to make a trial identification with the therapist as Oedipal mother in relation to the phantasied Oedipal father. The patient's wearing the skirt and blouse represented a step into the Oedipus complex proper, wherein the therapist's transference role was shifting from that of father-in-mother and mother-in-father to that of the mother identifying with the daughter in her Oedipal romance with the father. (In the countertransference, the therapist experienced affection and pride in response to the patient's silently asking for her loving blessing for the identification with the Oedipal mother, including her sexual and romantic interest in the Oedipal father.)

Following these developments, the patient's inhibition of her capacity for sexual fantasy diminished, allowing her to experience and take pleasure in genital-level sexual excitement, including masturbation. The sexual/ romantic fantasies of the "torrid affair" between herself (identified with Lauren Bacall) and Humphrey Bogart carried with it evidence of the continuing importance of the transitional Oedipal object. Bacall (as man-in-woman) was, in part, heir to the father-in-mother transference. However, in the Bogart–Bacall fantasy, there is a more fully triangulated object relationship (the patient, Bogart, and Bacall) in which the patient engages in an identification with (and enters into competition with) the external object mother—and thus (safely and pleasurably) enters into a romantic/sexual relationship with the Oedipal father as external object.

A Reevaluation of the Freudian Female Oedipal Narrative

At this point, Freud's narrative of the female Oedipus complex can be reexamined and perhaps better understood. From the perspective developed in this chapter, Freud's narrative of the female Oedipus complex (particularly his emphasis on the girl's turning to the father out of shame resulting from her awareness that she lacks a penis), can be viewed as an accurate description of a very common *pathological* outcome of female development and as a sub-theme of normal female development. When a girl's Oedipal experience unfolds in relation to a mother whose own unconscious Oedipal structure has undergone pathological development, the pathology will color the evolution of her daughter's Oedipal structure. For example, when the mother holds an unconscious belief that to be a female is to be flawed and shamefully lacking, it would be expected that her daughter would not only identify with this sense of shame and inner defectiveness, but would also feel narcissistically wounded at her mother's hands. In addition, it would be expected that the daughter, under these circumstances, would be angry and turn to her father in order to repair the narcissistic injury. The narcissistic wound is concretized in phantasy as a bodily wound, loss, or defect. The love of the father is needed to restore the little girl's self-esteem. The girl is dependent upon the love of her father (and later the love of other men) as a source of self-worth. Again, this is translated in unconscious phantasy into bodily terms wherein either the father's penis in intercourse or the father's baby is viewed as the thing that will complete the self. The excessive narcissism of women that Freud (1933) commented upon is not the inevitable outcome of female Oedipal development, but is frequently the outcome of pathological forms of the female Oedipus complex—for example, the result of a form of object relatedness arising as the result of a narcissistic wound incurred when the mother's unconscious conception of both herself and her daughter is that of shamefully incomplete human beings. Under such circumstances the girl will experience the "dress rehearsal" type of experience described earlier as the mother's act of grooming her daughter to attach herself to a man in order to complete herself.

Even when the mother unconsciously conceives of herself as lacking in the ways described, it is possible that the daughter may be able to utilize a less pathological (and less pathogenic) view held by her father (cf. Leonard, 1966). A healthy Oedipal romance with the father may provide an experience with someone who genuinely loves the little girl and conveys the feeling that he does not find her lacking. The daughter, if sufficiently resilient, is able to recognize and make use of this form of experience in shaping her emerging identity. However, the less secure child responds to this new experience by feeling that her self-esteem is dependent upon her father's unique ability to find her lovable, and that her value does not originate in any internal strength that she holds independent of his perception of her. In other words, she feels that it is her father who makes her special. This then leads in adolescence and adulthood to an addictive search for men who will make her feel special. The woman does not value her own capacities since they cannot provide her with a sense of value. Value originates in the man's act of finding her lovable. Under such circumstances, beauty literally lies in the eye of the beholder. Hence, such a woman is likely to develop a preoccupation with clothes, make-up, jewelry and the like, which are utilized for the purpose of attracting the attention of a man who will bring value to her through his love. This represents a special form of narcissistic disturbance since the patient is not looking for mirroring in the object; rather, she is hoping to revive a specific early love relationship in which her damaged self-esteem was rendered less painful through the influence of the love of her father. Her sense of injury was soothed by the father, but not completely repaired by it since his love was never sufficiently internalized as healthy narcissism.

One other aspect of the Freudian narrative can now be understood in a new light. Freud viewed the little girl's anger at her mother in the Oedipus complex as a reflection of the girl's blaming of her mother for not giving the little girl a penis, and thereby rendering the little girl incomplete and defective. From the perspective being developed in this chapter, the little girl's anger at her mother can be understood as a reflection of her feeling that the Oedipal mother, now experienced as far more external than before, has betrayed her in having a life of her own, and in particular in having a separate and private romantic and sexual life with the little girl's father.

Transference–Countertransference Implications

I would now like to describe a form of countertransference difficulty that is not uncommon in the psychoanalytic treatment of female patients. The countertransference problem that will be discussed seems to arise from an interplay of the patient's early Oedipal transferences (which are often externalized in the form of projective identifications [cf. Ogden, 1982b, 1983]) and the therapist's unanalyzed early Oedipal conflicts. (The principal focus here will be on the work of female therapists with female patients.) A major form of countertransference difficulty resulting from inadequacy of the transitional

Oedipal relationship[5] is an inability on the part of the female therapist to engage in a relatively unconflicted identification with her own father in her unconscious set of Oedipal object relationships. When the task of identifying with the unconscious Oedipal father must be defended against, the female therapist encounters great difficulty in conducting analytic therapy with patients whose transferences have their roots in the early Oedipal phase under discussion. The therapist who must defend against such an identification feels unconsciously hurt and angry about the idea of being asked to play a role that is transitional to an involvement with the Oedipal father. Such a therapist unconsciously feels that an effort on the part of the patient to make use of her in this way is a statement that she (the therapist) is second best, is lacking, is only a preliminary to "the real thing." The therapist unconsciously attempts to hold onto the patient, subtly or not so subtly conveying the feeling that it is a betrayal of the therapist for the patient to become involved with a man—even the therapist in the paternal transference. Under these circumstances the therapist feels so anxious about, and alienated from, her own identification with her father that she cannot recognize herself as the object of the paternal transference love. (See Searles, 1979, for a description of the therapist's jealousy of an internal object within himself or herself.) Such a therapist will often defensively attempt to foster a regression in the patient in order to avoid the identification

---

[5]The effort to describe transference manifestations of a given unconscious object relationship is of necessity very schematic since transferences are always overdetermined—that is, derived from a multiplicity of internal object relations at a variety of developmental levels.

under discussion. The therapist, for example, might "interpret downward" developmentally (for example, by interpreting genital-level material in oral terms) and in general treat the patient as if she were quite incapable of managing on her own. This is an expression of the therapist's unconscious wish to keep the patient a pre-Oedipal child forever in order to avoid entering into a triangulated Oedipal-level relationship with her that would require (among a great many other things) an identification with her own unconscious Oedipal father.

The therapist, when conflicted in this way, may unconsciously foster the patient's experience of the therapy as an alliance of two women against the world (unconsciously a male world, and more specifically, the world of the Oedipal father). The value system in the therapy moves in an unstated way toward the idea that the patient can "do it without men." The idea of maturity becomes unconsciously equated with complete self-sufficiency. The aid of the therapist or other women is not treated as a compromise of the patient's independence, because it is felt (unconsciously) that dependence on another woman is not an act of "selling out" to the enemy (the other, the Oedipal father). Here again, the patient experiences Oedipal love for the father (even in the transference) as a betrayal of the mother whose role is being unconsciously taken by the therapist. (The patient by means of projective identification often exerts great pressure on the therapist to experience herself in this way.) Since this aspect of the transference is being enacted by the therapist, it is left unanalyzed. At this juncture, there is often a disruption of treatment. The patient feels, but often cannot put into words, that she is being faced with an impossible choice — she may have either a father or a mother, but not both. Disruption, or threatened disruption, of the therapy is not so much an act of choosing the father over the mother as it is a refusal on the part of the patient to have to choose between the two. Patients being faced with this predicament in therapy regularly present dreams and screen memories in which impossible choices have to be made. (An example of such a dream is described later in this chapter.)

When a patient does not disrupt the therapy and decides to choose the jealous, possessive transference mother over the transference father, the therapist (as the transference mother) is experienced as a powerful phallic woman who has devoured the father and now possesses the penis. Instead of being experienced in the tranference as mother on-the-way-to-becoming father (the other), the therapist is experienced as a condensation of the powerful pre-Oedipal mother and what might have been, or used to be, the father. In the case of one therapy stalemated by such difficulties, transference to the therapist as phallic mother was represented by the patient in her fantasy that the therapist was a "man-eater" who had at one time shared her office suite with male therapists but had consumed them vaginally in the act of intercourse.

This fantasy stands in contrast to a transference to a therapist able to accept the transference role as transitional Oedipal mother (mother unconsciously identified with father). A patient represented this latter form of transference in a dream image of the therapist standing between two mirrors, in which the patient could see serial images of the therapist alternating with the image of an unrecognizable, but friendly and "familiar" man; the images extended infinitely backward. The man was "somehow also" the therapist.

Before closing this part of the discussion, I would like to briefly mention that the early Oedipal transferences being discussed play an equally important part in the work of male therapists treating female patients as they do in the work of female therapists treating female patients. In the case of the male therapist, a different, but related set of countertransference anxieties arises as he is cast in the role of the mother at this particular juncture in early Oedipal development. The male analyst may feel "left out," even though the patient is talking about being in love with a man who clearly has the characteristics of the analyst himself. The psychic reality underlying this observation is that the patient is in love with the father in the analyst-as-transference-mother, and not yet in love with the analyst as transference-father. Again, the analyst may feel jealous of another part of himself from which he may feel alienated because it requires that he experience himself as a woman (the mother identifying with her father). This early phase of the female Oedipus complex is easily overlooked in analyses conducted by male analysts because there is the continuity of the paternal element in both the developmentally earlier and later forms of transference: the developmentally earlier form involves the mother containing the father, whereas the developmentally later form involves a relationship with the father himself. (See Searles, 1959, for a discussion of Oedipal love in the countertransference as a necessary, but often very disturbing element of the work of male analysts with female patients manifesting Oedipal transferences.)

Implications for the Development of Gender Identity

The dilemma of having to choose between the mother and father (maleness and femaleness) that is generated by a mother's fear of engaging in an identification with her own father is at the core of many disorders of gender identity. From the point of view being developed here, the development of a healthy gender identity is a reflection of the creation of a dialectical interplay between masculine and feminine identities. This occurs when one does not have to choose between loving (and identifying with) one's mother and loving (and identifying with) one's father. Among the pivotal interpersonal experiences serving as a framework for this development is the Oedipal transitional relationship to the mother, in which the mother is male and female (mother-in-father and father-in-mother). In order for this experience to be generated, mother and daughter must be able to create and make use of a "play space" (Winnicott, 1971b,c) that both connects and separates them. The Oedipus complex is a drama to be played with in this space that is first created by the mother and daughter and later entered into by the father. If in the very beginning of the Oedipal phase, the question of who it is that the child is in love with (mother or father) must be answered, the play space "collapses" (Ogden, 1985b, 1986) and the Oedipal drama becomes all too real. The entry into the Oedipus complex under such circumstances involves an impossible choice.

A patient struggling with the terror of this choice (brought to life in the transference) presented a dream in which she was standing in the aisle of an airplane that was about to crash. The patient had to sit either with her mother on one side of the aisle or with her father on the other side. The patient knew that whoever she sat with would survive and that the other parent would die. The patient understood this dream as representing a choice that she felt she had to make in which the outcome would be that half of herself would die.

When the choice has to be made between mother and father (between maleness and femaleness), one becomes neither masculine nor feminine since in healthy masculinity and healthy femininity each depends upon, and is created by, the other. This is part of the implication of Freud's (1905, 1925, 1931) insistence on the fundamental bisexuality of human beings.

Disorders of gender identity can be understood as disturbances of the intrapsychic dialectical relationship of masculinity and femininity. An attempt to make the painful (matricidal or patricidal, and always suicidal) choice leads to the construction of a pseudo-identity. Examples of such pseudo-identities are seen in the lesbian caricature of masculinity ("the dyke") and the male homosexual's caricature of femininity ("the queen"). Such brittle pseudo-identities lack the subtle resonance of the masculinity and femininity that characterize mature gender identity. The triangulation that is the outcome of a satisfactory Oedipal transitional relationship represents a restructuring of the individual's fundamental bisexuality in such a way that femininity need not be a flight from, or denial of, masculinity (and vice versa).

Summary

The concept of the Oedipal transitional relationship is proposed as a way of understanding the nature of the psychological-interpersonal process mediating the little girl's entry into the Oedipus complex. This transitional relationship serves to allow the little girl to nontraumatically discover the father as external object in the context of the safety of the dyadic relationship to the mother. In this early phase of Oedipal development, the little girl falls in love with the mother-as-father and the father-as-mother—that is, falls in love with the mother in her unconscious identification with her (the mother's) own father. In this way, paradoxically, the first triangulated object relationship is experienced in a two-person relationship; the first heterosexual relationship develops in a relationship involving two females; the father as libidinal object is discovered in the mother.

6

The Threshold of the Male Oedipus Complex

The Oedipus complex was in many ways for Freud the centerpiece of psychoanalytic theory. He saw in it the convergence of universal psychological structure, unconscious personal meaning, and the influence of the power of desire emanating from the body. As a result, the Oedipus complex has properly occupied a central position in analytic thinking for more than ninety years.[1] In this chapter, I shall limit my focus to an aspect of the Oedipus complex that I believe has heretofore been a relatively neglected part of the analytic discourse concerning early Oedipal development.

Although it is generally agreed that the transition into the Oedipus complex represents a critical juncture in psychological development, I believe that psychoanalytic theory has not yet sufficiently elaborated a conception of

[1]Freud discussed the importance of the ideas constituting the Oedipus complex in his October 15, 1897, letter to Fliess, but did not use the term *Oedipus complex* in his publications until 1910.

the psychological-interpersonal processes mediating this transition in male development. In this chapter, I shall propose that the transition into the male Oedipus complex is mediated by a transitional relationship with the mother, analogous to that seen in female development (cf. Chapter 5), but with a significant difference in emphasis. This difference is a consequence of the fact that the Oedipal mother is and is not the same mother the little boy loved, hated, and feared prior to his discovery of her (and his father) as external Oedipal objects. The complications caused by the psychological proximity of the pre-Oedipal and Oedipal love objects (in the positive Oedipus complex) are specific to male development, and necessitate a psychological solution that is distinctive to the development of the boy. Essential to the resolution of the problem resulting from the coincidence of the object of the little boy's pre-Oedipal and Oedipal love is the role of the primal scene phantasy[2] as an unconscious organizer of evolving sexual meaning and personal identity.[3]

---

[2]The term *primal scene phantasy* refers to a group of conscious and unconscious phantasies on the theme of observed parental intercourse. These phantasies are characterized by varying degrees of primitivity, a range of modes of object relatedness, different forms and intensities of identification with each of the figures in the phantasy, and so on.

[3]In female development, there are overlapping but not identical psychological difficulties at the threshold of the Oedipus complex. For example, identification with the mother at this juncture inevitably carries with it the pull toward more primitive wishes to be at one with her (as opposed to simply being like her). It is beyond the scope of this chapter to discuss the role of primal scene phantasies in facilitating the little girl's differentiation of herself from her Oedipal and pre-Oedipal mother(s), her acknowledgment of sexual and generational difference, and the development of the female Oedipus complex.

This set of phantasies (primal scene phantasies) carries with it in both male and female development a powerful sense of thirdness. The space between mother and child provided by the Other (the third) allows for the elaboration of symbol formation proper, subjectivity, and the compromise of personal omnipotence that is involved in the discovery of externality and the recognition of sexual and generational difference. The movement into the male Oedipus complex necessarily involves a psychological state in which the externality of the Oedipal-object mother is continually in danger of being blurred by the shadow cast by the pre-Oedipal mother. The psychological task of this phase of development for the boy is not the renunciation of the pre-Oedipal mother, but the establishment of a dialectical tension between pre-Oedipal and Oedipal love relationships with the mother.

Freud's Perspective

Despite the fact that Freud (1925, 1931) understood the importance of the psychological movement into the Oedipus complex, he did not seem to recognize the nature of the unconscious conflict inherent in this transition for the boy. "In both cases [that is, for boys and for girls] the mother is the original object; and *it is no surprise* that boys retain the object in the Oedipus complex" (Freud, 1925, p. 251, italics added).

I believe that Freud was not able to adequately conceptualize the nature of the psychological problems faced by the boy in retaining his mother as love object in the Oedipus complex, because he (Freud) had only begun to develop an understanding of internal object relations in general and of the pre-Oedipal relationship of the little boy to his mother in particular.[4]

Freud (1921) proposed that for boys, the construction of an Oedipus complex involves an "irresistible advance toward unification" (p. 105) of two initially independent facets of psychological life: the boy's sexual tie to his mother and his idealization of his father. He further believed that primal scene phantasies play an essential role in the "pre-history" of the Oedipus complex. Freud understood primal scene phantasies to be universal, and therefore felt that it is not reasonable to assume that they arise from actual experience of witnessing parental intercourse. Rather, he understood these phantasies to be part of a group of phylogenetically inherited "primal phantasies" (Freud, 1916–1917), in other words, to be biologically passed-on portions of the experience of the species.

> I believe [that in these primal phantasies] . . . the individual reaches beyond his own experience into primaeval experience at points where his own experience has been too rudimentary. It seems to me quite possible that all the things that are told us today in analysis as phantasy — the seduction of children, the inflaming of sexual excitement by observing

---

[4]Freud (1925, 1933) began to formulate a conception of the pre-Oedipal relationship between the little girl and her mother in the course of attempting to understand what he believed to be the little girl's angry rejection of her mother at the threshold of the Oedipus complex. "We cannot understand women unless we appreciate this phase of their pre-Oedipus attachment to their mother" (Freud, 1933, p. 119). However, Freud continued to believe that the pre-Oedipal relationship between mother and child held significantly less importance in the development of the boy than in that of the girl (cf. Laplanche and Pontalis, 1967).

parental intercourse, the threat of castration (or rather castration itself) — were once real occurrences in the primaeval times of the human family, and that children in their phantasies are simply filling in the gaps in individual truth with prehistoric truth. [pp. 370–371]

As I have previously discussed (Ogden, 1984), this does not mean that a given phantasy (a set of thoughts and feelings) is inherited; instead, there is a structural, psychological readiness to organize experience along specific, predetermined lines. I have termed this form of structure *psychological deep structure* and view it as analogous to linguistic deep structure as described by Chomsky (1957, 1968). Although Freud viewed primal scene phantasies as part of the pre-history of the Oedipus complex, he did not elaborate his conception of the way this group of phantasies influences the development of the Oedipus complex. Although Freud is often accused of dealing inadequately with the problems of female sexual development, I believe that he gave less attention to the problem of the little boy's entry into the Oedipus complex than he did to the problem of the entry into the female Oedipus complex. I concur with Freud's acknowledgment, "As regards the pre-history of the Oedipus complex in boys, we are far from complete clarity" (1925, p. 250).

In light of understandings of pre-Oedipal internal and external object relationships that have been developed over the past forty years (see, for example, Bion, 1962; Chasseguet-Smirgel, 1984a; Fairbairn, 1952; Jacobson, 1964; Kernberg, 1976; Klein, 1975; Kohut, 1971; Lewin, 1950; Mahler, 1968; Searles, 1966; Spitz, 1965; Stern, 1985; Winnicott, 1958), it is no longer sufficient to simply assert that "it is no surprise that boys retain [the mother as] . . . object in the Oedipus complex"

(Freud, 1925). On the contrary, I believe that there are salient reasons for the boy *not* to retain his mother as Oedipal object. In addition to the psychological conflicts intrinsic to the Oedipus complex (such as the incest taboo and aggressive wishes toward loved objects), the boy must take an object he had experienced as omnipotent and only partially differentiated from himself as the focus of his romantic and sexual wishes and phantasies. Rather than viewing the boy's Oedipal object choice as simply inevitable, I believe that we must ask "How is it possible for the little boy to take his mother as the object of his Oedipal love, and what are the psychological-interpersonal processes mediating the transition from the pre-Oedipal to the Oedipal relationship with the mother?"

Although analytic theory has addressed a great many aspects of the preconditions of the Oedipus complex, such as the role of primal scene phantasies (Chasseguet-Smirgel, 1984b; Green, 1983; McDougall, 1980, 1986), the timing of the onset of Oedipal object relations (Bibring, 1947; Galenson and Roiphe, 1974; Heimann, 1971; Klein, 1928; Parens et al., 1976; Sachs, 1977), and structural antecedents of the Oedipus complex (Fairbairn, 1952; Klein, 1952b; Winnicott, 1960b), the analytic discourse has not included a thorough discussion of the psychological and interpersonal processes that mediate the boy's entry into the Oedipus complex.

The Scylla and Charybdis of the Threshold of the Male Oedipus Complex

The little boy's relationship with the pre-Oedipal mother constitutes a critical and problematic precondition of the

Oedipus complex. The entry into an erotic and romantic relationship with the Oedipal mother is fraught with anxiety in part because she bears an uncanny resemblance to the omnipotent pre-Oedipal mother. For the girl, the preponderance of the psychological problem involved in the change of object at the threshold of the Oedipus complex lies in her task of nontraumatically making a transition from a relationship to an internal object to a love relationship with an external object whom the little girl has not yet met and cannot omnipotently control (Ogden, 1985a). Thus, the danger for the girl lies in large part in making a leap into the abyss of externality that lies beyond her omnipotent control. As I discussed in Chapter 5, this risk is made bearable by means of a transitional Oedipal relationship to a "father-in-mother" and "mother-in-father" wherein the question of whether the little girl is engaged in a relationship with her (Oedipal) father or with her (pre-Oedipal) mother never arises. As in other forms of transitional phenomena, an area of illusion is created in the transitional mother–daughter relationship, wherein the relationship is to both the (known) mother and the (yet-to-be-known, external object) father. There is a hardness-in-softness (a father-in-mother) that allows the father to be simultaneously created and discovered, thus making possible the leap of faith involved in the little girl's falling in love with her father whom she has not yet met as an external object.

For the little boy, there is a dual psychological problem in which the distribution of psychological danger is different from that encountered by the girl at the threshold of the Oedipus complex. The danger in the boy's entry into the Oedipus complex does not lie only in the fact that the Oedipal mother (and father) are dangerously external and therefore unknown, unpredictable, and uncontrollable. What makes this psychological juncture complex in a way that is distinctive to the little boy is the fact that he must struggle to create distance between himself and the powerful pre-Oedipal mother while he falls in love with the Oedipal mother. He has known the pre-Oedipal mother as a primitive, omnipotent, partially differentiated object by whom he has been mesmerized and penetrated, whom he has ruthlessly used and omnipotently destroyed and recreated (Winnicott, 1954). She also has the glow of warmth and safety that makes him "dissolve" in a way that is both blissful and terrifying at the same time, since this "dissolution" causes him to begin to lose touch with his accruing knowledge of where he stops and where she begins.

The Organization of Sexual Meaning

The task of the early Oedipal period in male development is that of safely negotiating a passage between the danger of the traumatic discovery of otherness and the danger of experiencing the Oedipal romance as overwhelmingly dominated by the shadow of the pre-Oedipal mother. This journey between the Scylla of the external-Oedipal-object mother and the Charybdis of the omnipotent pre-Oedipal mother is in part mediated by the power of primal scene phantasies to organize sexual meaning and identity. From this perspective, primal scene phantasies are not simply an exciting combination of sexual and aggressive thoughts about parental intercourse; rather, they are pivotal organizers of internal and external object relations that will come to constitute the mature Oedipus complex.

The primal scene phantasy in its role as organizer of evolving sexual meaning and identity is by no means a static entity. Rather, it is a constellation of thoughts and feelings in which the form of object relatedness, the degree of subjectivity, the modes of defense, and the maturity and complexity of affect are all in a state of evolution and flux. The image of observed parental intercourse serves as a mold, a way of thinking about the unthinkable. The objects constituting the phantasy are in the beginning predominantly part-objects engaged in frightening battle that involves mysterious sexuality intermingled with violence. There is initially very little of an interpreting subject in the experiencing of these phantasies; rather, there is predominantly a self-as-object who is *part of the scene* with almost no sense of being removed from it, much less a sense of being an observing subject capable of thinking about and understanding (interpreting) one's response to it. Nonetheless, there is always a rudimentary sense of thirdness inherent in the structure of the primal scene phantasy.

The more primitive versions of the primal scene phantasy constituting the early edges of Oedipal experience are cast in a predominantly paranoid-schizoid mode:[5] the boy is part of a sexual/aggressive event that has the quality of an intense sensory experience in which

---

[5]In brief, I use the term *paranoid-schizoid mode* to refer to a mode of generating experience characterized by (1) a very limited capacity to experience oneself as the author and interpreter of one's thoughts and feelings; (2) a form of symbolization in which the symbol is barely distinguishable from the symbolized ("symbolic equation," Segal, 1957); (3) part-object relatedness; and (4) the use of omnipotent thinking, splitting, and projective identification in the service of defense and the organization of experience. (See Chapter 2 and Ogden, 1986, for further discussion of the paranoid-schizoid mode.)

he is immersed. The quality of this form of experience was vividly captured by a patient in his third year of analysis. The patient presented a screen memory in which he, as a 7-year-old, "groped around" in his parents' bedroom for the light switch of the floor lamp next to their bed and accidentally put his fingers into the socket from which the bulb was missing. Waves of a strange vibratory sensation that he had never before felt or even imagined went through his body. He had no idea what was happening, but the experience was so powerful that he "knew" it would kill him if it did not stop within a few seconds. He felt that he had no control over his body or his sphincters and could not remove his hand from the opening. The patient reported that he had had the distinct feeling of being caught between two "things." He later made sense of this feeling by conceiving of the two "things" as the socket and the lamp-stand. He felt as if he had become part of it (them), as if he were a piece of the apparatus holding the two together. However, at the time, there was no "as if" quality to the experience — he was part of this intense force connecting the (penis-like) lamp-stand to the (vagina-like) socket.

This screen memory represents a psychological construction built upon an unconscious primal scene phantasy of a relatively primitive type. There is the feeling of something dangerous happening of which the patient became a part and from which he could not extricate himself. There was barely the sense of a self with the capability of thinking and acting — and what little there was of such a self was felt to be dissolving into nothing (the fear of being killed in the intensity of the experience).

In the patient's analysis it came to be understood that this screen memory represented an attempt at creating a narrative to contain the terrifying and overly exciting unconscious primal scene phantasies with which he, as a child, had been grappling. In the particular screen memory that was generated, the patient was omnipotently identified with the sexual force connecting the mother and father, the penis and the vagina. Perhaps more accurately stated, he had become that force. In this way, the patient was not excluded from the sexual act; he was the power in it. Psychically, this patient experienced himself as *being* the power (the dangerous, disintegrating, exciting, connecting force) in the sexual act, and only later was he able to attempt to *possess* that sexual power.[6]

Even in such primitive versions of the primal scene phantasy, there is an element of thirdness (for example, in the patient's tenuously held capacity to observe and describe the experience). This thirdness holds the potential to become in the course of development the fully triangulated object relations that characterize more mature versions of the primal scene phantasy and of the Oedipus complex itself.[7]

---

[6]Lacan (1956–1957, 1958) has commented on the movement in male development from the unmediated sense of being the phallus (for the Other) to the symbolically mediated experience of having a phallus.

[7]In both female and male development, the primal scene phantasy, even in its primitive forms, serves as an important vehicle for the creation of thirdness. The thirdness provided by primal scene phantasies seems to have differing significance in male and in female development. For the boy the mother as object of Oedipal desire is continually in danger of being eroded by his attachment to the pre-Oedipal mother (cf. Stoller, 1973). Since for the little girl there is an actual change of object, the erosion of the otherness *of the object* of Oedipal desire poses a somewhat lesser threat. However, in female development, there is the danger of the collapse of the little girl's mature Oedipal *identification* with her mother, into a primitive sense of merger with the pre-Oedipal mother (cf. Chodorow, 1978). This

Transitional Oedipal Object Relatedness

For the little boy (as well as for the little girl), the transition from paranoid-schizoid versions of the primal scene phantasy into the mature Oedipus complex is psychologically and interpersonally mediated by a relationship with the mother that is similar to, but developmentally later than, the relationship to transitional objects described by Winnicott (1951). Paradoxically, it is through a relationship with the mother, a female, that the little boy acquires a phallus;[8] it is in the context of a dyadic relationship with the mother that Oedipal triangulation develops; it is in a relationship with a woman that the boy's male identification and paternal idealization originate.

The little boy encounters phallic thirdness within the transitional Oedipal relationship to the mother. In this relationship the mother is simultaneously experienced as

---

represents a psychological danger for the little girl that is somewhat analogous to, and yet distinctly different from, the collapse of the Oedipal mother (as love object) into the pre-Oedipal mother in male development. The differences between these forms of psychological danger in part determine the different ways in which primal scene phantasies are elaborated and made use of in male and female development.

[8] The little boy is born with a penis, but this is not to say that he is born with a phallus. The former is an anatomical structure; the latter is a set of symbolic meanings that the boy comes to attribute to his sense of himself as a male in general, and to his psychic representation of his penis in particular. It is through the development of the capacity to attribute phallic significance to himself that the little boy becomes empowered sexually. (Since a phallus and a penis are not equivalent, little girls similarly develop phallic significance for themselves in their sense of generativity, sexual potency, power-in-the-world, and the like.)

father-in-mother and mother-in-father. The question of which is the case is never asked. It is the mother's set of unconscious internal Oedipal object relations that is the framework within which the Oedipal transitional relationship with the little boy develops. The mother brings the phallic father to the emerging Oedipal relationship with her son through her own internal Oedipal father, with whom she is identified.

The absence of a firmly established internal object father in the mother's unconscious Oedipal object relations generates an emotional vacuum that robs the little boy of one of the essential ingredients with which to psychologically and interpersonally elaborate the Oedipus complex. The actual father is only secondarily the bearer of the phallus with which the little boy will identify in the process of generating phallic significance for himself. In the beginning, there is no such thing as a mother and infant due to the presence of the father imago in the mother's unconscious mind (cf. Green, 1975).

The mother's unconscious Oedipus complex involves a reverberating, mutually enriching set of object relations in which the mother is simultaneously a little girl in love with her father, her father in love with his daughter, a mother in love with her husband, a mother and father protectively guarding generational boundaries. (These object relations are of course only a small sample of the multitude of internal object relations constituting the unconscious Oedipus complex.) The mother who is identified with each of these internal objects is psychologically drawn upon in different ways by her son in the course of their evolving relationship.[9] At the threshold of the

---

[9]Since each child draws upon his or her mother's unconscious in different ways, no two children have the same mother.

Oedipus complex, the mother is both the internal object father who sexually empowers the boy, as well as the external object mother who is the object of the boy's sexual desire. This configuration is captured in "a common fantasy of little children" (McDougall, 1986, p. 26): the child imagines himself lying "between the two parents, during which time the father puts his penis into the little boy who then develops a strong penis that can go into his mother" (p. 26).

The paradox of masculinity-in-femininity, of third-ness-in-twoness, that is at the heart of the transitional Oedipal relationship comes to constitute a new version of the primal scene phantasy as the little boy begins to enter into more mature Oedipal object relations. At this juncture, the primal scene phantasy is developed into a narrative of the observation of the father and the mother in the act of sexual intercourse. The transitional Oedipal mother, who had in a paradoxical manner embodied the father-in-the-mother and the mother-in-the-father, now becomes elaborated as a figure in a narrative in which father and mother are more distinctly differentiated and then joined together in the act of sexual intercourse. In other words, sexual difference is for the first time clearly acknowledged and at the same time a new unity is created: the unity of the child's knowledge of sexual intercourse involving two parents, each different from the other, and each distinct from himself. In this more differentiated version of the primal scene phantasy, the little boy no longer experiences himself as the embodiment of sexual excitement in a world of part objects; rather, he is now a subject in a world of whole objects who experiences the sexual excitement of having a phallus, and who—through a more mature identification with his father—takes his mother as the object of his love and sexual desire. The fact that he is at the same time "only" the observer of the sexual act sufficiently separates him from the danger of actual incest, which would threaten him with the loss of his identity. (It is important to emphasize that what is at stake is not merely castration, but annihilation through the collapse of one's sense of self as it is subsumed by the mother [cf. Loewald, 1979].)

There is an important (but not altogether welcomed) reminder in this new version of the primal scene phantasy that the little boy is, after all, his mother's son, not his mother's husband; that he is, in reality, emotionally and sexually immature while his mother and father are emotionally and sexually mature; that he is his father's son and is not the father himself. These ambivalently experienced reminders of external reality help the little boy maintain the primal scene phantasy in a potential space in which unconscious thinking can occur as opposed to hallucination and delusion. Excessively eroticized object relations with the mother render these phantasies indistinguishable from reality. Under such circumstances psychotic identification ("I am my father") replaces mature identification ("I am like my father").[10]

---

[10]Psychological development is short-circuited when overly sexualized object relations between mother and son lead the little boy to delusionally experience his growing up as a magical process brought about by means of omnipotent wishes. This stands in contrast to a normal sense of the process of growing up as being a gradual one, in which one learns and develops over time on the basis of object-related experience and slowly maturing bodily and psychological processes. Such a short-circuiting of development, leading to a hypertrophy of omnipotent thinking, occurs both under circumstances in which actual incest has occurred as well as circumstances in which a

Clinical Illustration

I would now like to briefly describe portions of an analysis in which the transference–countertransference phenomena shed light on a form of early difficulty in the transition into the male Oedipus complex.

Dr. L., a 36-year-old biochemist, began analysis because he experienced himself as destined to spend his life being "pretty good, but not great at anything." He had had hopes of becoming a university professor of chemistry, but had done little to bring this about. Upon completing his doctoral studies in biochemistry he had accepted the first job offered to him by a recruiter for a pharmaceutical company. Similarly, he had married the first woman who appeared to love him and who wanted to marry him. It seemed beyond belief to Dr. L. that any woman would want to marry him. He had two sons, but said that it did not feel as if they were his sons and that he did not know what it felt like to be a father. (He later disclosed fantasies that his children had been conceived during affairs that he imagined his wife had had.)

Dr. L. was preoccupied by the idea that he had a small penis. He would never take a shower in a men's locker room nor would he use a urinal in a public lavatory. Initially, he was concerned that the truth that analysis would reveal would be "the fact" that he was gay. He equated the idea of having a small penis with the idea of being gay. Dr. L. explained that he had never been sexually attracted to men and that the idea of actually having sex with a man revolted him. He confessed that he

---

sexualized *folie à deux* has resulted in a shared belief that mother and son have succeeded in creating a marriage that has eliminated the Other.

had had a few homosexual dreams, but quickly added
that he had read that this was "normal."

The analysis was remarkable for the striking lack of
psychological-mindedness demonstrated by this analysand. Dr. L. was a patient who seemed to be trying
extremely hard to be a good patient, but despite — or
perhaps because of — his best efforts he came up with a
pale imitation of insight. He arrived at my office day
after day to toil away at analysis and asked for no help
from me, nor did he seem to expect any. Very gradually
it became clear that the patient did not anticipate that a
dialogue of any kind would take place between us.

About a year into the analysis, I told the patient that
I thought that he had little hope of the two of us ever
really talking to one another, and that he had even less
hope of anything changing during the course of analysis.
Dr. L. was taken by surprise by these comments, saying
that it had never even occurred to him that we would ever
talk to one another. Why would I want to talk to him? He
said it was also true that he had never had much hope that
the analysis would be of any value to him and he admitted
that he had actually consulted me only at his wife's
urging. Dr. L. said that he had thought I would not agree
to work with him if he told me in the beginning that he
had no expectation of getting anything out of our work
together. The patient seemed relieved that his "real" view
of things could be "placed on the table in such an
ungarnished way." This image elicited my own fantasy of
the patient as an ungarnished slab of meat thrown on a
dinner plate (the couch) in abject passivity and utterly
lacking in appeal. I began to get a more immediate sense
of the way in which the only safety this person could
secure for himself was the safety of being someone who
expected and desired nothing. Any remnant of his ca-

pacity for desire was to be carried by other people—his wife, his children, job recruiters, and now me.

Dr. L.'s mother was described as a woman who was contemptuous of the patient's father because he had failed to earn as much money as her friends' husbands earned. She continually compared him with her own father who had been a very wealthy businessman, saying that her father had "genuinely" loved his family and that it had always been important to him that they feel proud of how they lived, the house they lived in, the way they dressed, and so on.

Dr. L. described his own father as a well-meaning man who was unable to stand up to his wife. He seemed to "plead guilty as accused" most of the time, although he would occasionally fight back when being harped at by his wife.

Following the interpretation of his hopelessness about achieving anything in analysis, Dr. L. diminished his effort to imitate the way he imagined someone else might behave in analysis. In its place there developed a profound feeling of pointlessness. I commented that he seemed to feel that he had no idea of how to make use of me or of analysis, and that as a result he felt nothing was happening or was likely to happen. But his experience of despair represented an important shift in the analysis: for the first time it felt to me as if there were two people in the room who were experiencing feelings that felt real and could be given names that seemed accurate. Nonetheless, due to Dr. L.'s sense of extreme alienation from me (his sense that he did not know what he was doing in my office), there was an almost complete absence of a feeling of two people meeting together to do a piece of work.

Dr. L. talked enviously of his friends who "worshiped" or "despised" their analysts; he did not understand their passions. The patient said that he could not see me as any different from anybody else: "You get into your pants one foot at a time." This conscious and unconscious phantasy of me without my pants captured the patient's experience of me as the antithesis of a sexual, phallic presence. In the unconscious phantasy I was inserting my penis into a vagina (my foot into my trouser leg), and yet both the experience of phallic power and the danger of intercourse were eliminated by reducing the act to the most banal, mundane activity possible. In addition, since both the degraded penis and the vagina were mine, the phantasy was of my having intercourse with myself. In this way he refused to acknowledge sexual difference, or to own or to assign sexual power. (The patient's lack of insightfulness had similarly created an interpersonal enactment in which neither he nor I was empowered phallically.)

With this background, I will now focus on a portion of the analytic work that took place in the third year of analysis. In the course of the first two years of analysis the patient had developed a significantly different vantage point from which to view his own and his mother's childhood relationships. He said that he had formerly thought of his mother and her father (his grandfather) as having had a very special relationship with one another. The patient's grandfather had seemed to be so powerful and godlike for his mother that "no other man could possibly replace him in her pantheon." He said that he now thought of that relationship as involving a very strange idealization of his grandfather by his mother. The patient had, in the course of analysis, developed intense curiosity about the relationship between his mother and grandfather. As a result, he had spoken with his maternal aunt and uncle about their childhood experiences. The voyeuristic pleasure that he derived from his "detective work" was referred to by Dr. L. as "my morbid fascination with my mother's 'other life.' "

Dr. L. came to view his mother's worship of her father as her unconscious effort to deny the fact that she had felt quite neglected by him. The patient's grandfather was, as far as the patient could gather, an extremely narcissistic man who paid very little attention to his children or to his wife. When he was at home, he insisted on absolute quiet. His weekends were spent at his club. The children ate separately from their parents and were sent to their floor of the house before he arrived home. This arrangement continued until the children were adolescents and were thought to be old enough to maintain the silence and decorum that the father required. Dr. L. was aware of the satisfaction he was taking in constructing this version of his mother's family story.

In the same period of the analysis, the patient reported with a profound sense of shame a masturbatory fantasy (more accurately, a set of fantasies involving variations on an unchanging central theme) that had formed a major part of his fantasy life from as early as he could remember. Dr. L. said that he had hoped he would be able to "get through analysis" without ever talking to me about this part of his life. However, he felt that there was now no alternative to discussing it because he was being plagued by intrusive thoughts of having anal intercourse with me. He was extremely anxious that the fact that he was having these thoughts meant that he was gay. He felt out of control in a way that he had never before experienced and was afraid that his difficulty in concentrating would lead to his losing his job.

In these masturbatory fantasies, which dated from childhood, the patient could hear his mother calling him from her darkened bedroom. Her voice is sweet and inviting, but it has a "timbre" that he has never before heard from her so he is not certain that it really is she. He suspects that she may be possessed by creatures from outer space. He feels both excited and frightened, and wishes that his father were there to go in and see what is happening and tell the patient if it really is his mother and whether it is safe to go in. He feels that he might be killed by whatever it is in the room if he were to go in by himself. However, he does not feel that he can leave his mother alone in there because he does not want her to be hurt or killed by whatever it is that has taken control of her. He feels that he must choose between saving his own life and trying to save his mother's. He cannot choose and is paralyzed by the tension. At the same time, he wonders if he is lingering in order to hear the wonderfully exciting sound that is coming from the bedroom.

The introduction of this set of phantasies into the analytic discourse represented a second turning point in the analysis. It was followed by a piece of enactment of the transference that further elaborated the unconscious themes of the patient's masturbatory phantasies. Dr. L. began to experience an urgent need to get his wife into analysis, and he insistently, repeatedly, and at times pleadingly asked me for the name of an analyst she might consult. In our discussion of the phantasy underlying this request/demand, it became clear that the patient had in mind a "senior, male analyst," someone "who has been around for a while and knows what he is doing." (This description stood in stark contrast to the patient's experience of me at the time.) Dr. L. threatened to disrupt the analysis if I would not comply with his demand. The patient's awareness that he could have gone to several other people for the names of analysts for his wife did not in the least diminish the tenacity with which he sought my participation in the enactment of this internal drama.

I told Dr. L. that I thought he felt hopelessly trapped by me in the analysis, as if he had no escape from my web other than somehow finding a way of getting a father into the room to see what was going on. The patient responded by saying that he felt as if he no longer knew who I was, what I wanted with him, or how he would ever be able to leave me and lead his own life. His wish that I give him a referral for his wife was eventually understood by the patient as an unconscious attempt to create a family by getting me (the transference pre-Oedipal mother) to take a "real" (phallic Oedipal) husband who could be a "real father." (In addition, there was a paternal transference in which he experienced me as unable to be that "real father.") He later told me that I seemed so much like a woman to him that he thought he had smelled female genital odors in my bathroom, which he had associated with me. He said that he had begun to feel panicky when he anticipated coming to my office, imagining it to be a room so small that he would not be able to breathe. (He had had an elevator phobia as a child and for years would climb many flights of stairs in order to avoid using elevators.)

The patient then described in more detail something to which he had only vaguely alluded earlier in the analysis: from latency onward he had masturbated while wearing his mother's underwear, and, after he married, had continued this practice with his wife's underwear. Dr. L. said that at these times he imagined himself to be his mother with a penis, masturbating. I said to him that in this fantasy he did not need a father to go into the bedroom with him since in this scene he was his mother: there were no fathers, no sons, no differences between men and women; everything had collapsed into a single person, a single sex.

Dr. L. in this masturbatory fantasy had created a delusional sexual identity with his mother, since the only sexuality that exists in the fantasy (in the absence of a phallic father) is a form of female sexuality that has subsumed what might have become masculinity. The phallic third seems to have been only tenuously present in the patient's mother's unconscious Oedipal object relations. The mother's defensively idealized father seems to have been only a shadow of a vital Oedipal object. Dr. L.'s own father could not fully compensate for the insufficiently present Oedipal father in the mother's unconscious mind. (No external object can fully substitute for a fragile internal object.) In this phase of analysis, the patient was able to understand the way in which neither his mother nor he could make use of his father: the actual father was reduced to the status of an inadequate replacement for a wished-for Oedipal father who had barely existed in the mother's unconscious mind. The potential for a transitional Oedipal relationship to a father-in-mother seems to have collapsed into a delusional relationship to a sexualized pre-Oedipal mother who served to deny sexual difference.

In the course of the analytic work, Dr. L. began to view his father as having strengths that he had not previously valued. He came to feel that his father need not be viewed simply as a man without ambition; from another point of view, one that the patient had never before considered, he began to see his father as a man who did not care very much about either social status or material possessions. Dr. L. said that his father cared deeply about political causes that had been dismissed by the patient's mother as at best quixotic and at worst a self-indulgent waste of time that took his attention away from the "real world" of money and business. His father in the 1950s had, at considerable risk to himself, hired black employees for responsible positions when almost no other whites in their Southern city were doing so. This aspect of his father, although obviously present from the beginning of the patient's life, was not previously utilizable for purposes of identification by the patient. The patient said that there was something very sad about his relationship with his father: it was not a matter of his not having had a father, but a case of his not having recognized the fact that he did have one. He said he not only deeply regretted having missed out on having had a fuller relationship with his father; he felt even worse about the fact that he had cheated his father out of the experience of feeling like a father.

In the paternal transference, Dr. L. for the first time became able to feel love for me without immediately becoming anxious that both he and I had become women or homosexuals in the process. This anxiety had previously taken the form of intrusive thoughts of having anal intercourse with me. If the only sexuality that exists is the consuming maternal sexuality imagined by the patient, then there could be no loving relationship with, or sexual identification with, another man that does not ultimately reveal itself to be "homosexual" (that is, a sexuality devoid of phallic thirdness). For this patient, homosexuality was a reflection of the phallic father having been subsumed by the mother, leaving only a degraded sexuality devoid of masculinity. As these feelings were experienced and interpreted in the transference, the intrusive "homosexual" thoughts receded.

Although Dr. L. had heard from friends that I wrote

books and articles, he had never read any of them, fearing that he would either not like or not understand them. In other words, he had feared that his response would be to reduce either himself or me to a degraded state. At this point in the analysis, Dr. L. did read one of my books and said that his reaction surprised him: he felt proud of me. He said that he had never before felt proud of anything of his own, or of anyone with whom he was associated.

The Absence of Thirdness

As illustrated by the material presented from Dr. L.'s analysis, an impoverished identification of a boy's mother with her own father results in a sense (for the boy) of a missing Other (i.e., a missing father-in-mother). The little boy then finds himself psychologically alone with his Oedipal mother, and this fact profoundly influences several aspects of his development. First, there is very little sense of a phallic presence with which to identify, and therefore a scarcity of opportunity to become phallically empowered. Secondly, the little boy is not insulated by the protective prohibition of the phallic third (the father-in-mother) who claims his wife as his own object of love and sexual desire and thus helps to delineate a generational boundary. The act of protective prohibition ordinarily provided by the father (initially the father-in-mother) is of critical value to the little boy in warding off the catastrophic feeling that he may actually have his bluff called and be invited into a real sexual union with his mother. Without the protectively prohibiting father-in-mother with whom to identify, the primal scene phantasy becomes terrifying and must be defended against by means of perverse[11] sexual solutions. The primal scene phantasy, in the absence of a father-in-mother, is a phantasy of intercourse with the omnipotent mother of unmediated two-ness. However, in addition, this mother has begun to take on the terrifying strangeness of genital female sexuality. This female sexuality is not made safe by a father-in-mother, a phallus within the vagina (the mother's identification with her own father). Unopposed female sexuality becomes a frightening caricature of sexuality for the boy in that it is marked by the absence of the father who in phantasy has been destroyed by the mother (cf. McDougall, 1982). It is sexuality inseparable from the catastrophe of the destruction of the phallic father, and therefore a sexuality that blocks the little boy's entrance into sexual and emotional maturity and the achievement of mature masculine gender identity.

Summary

In this chapter, I have proposed that the entry into the male Oedipus complex is mediated by the development of a transitional Oedipal object relationship in conjunction with the elaboration of increasingly mature forms of the primal scene phantasy. In the transitional Oedipal relationship in male development, the mother is experienced simultaneously as the omnipotent pre-Oedipal mother, the sexually exciting external object mother, and

---

[11]I use the term "perverse" to refer to forms of sexuality that are used in the service of denying the separateness of external objects and sexual difference, and thus interfere with the elaboration of the depressive position (cf. McDougall, 1986).

(through the mother's unconscious identification with her own father) the phallic Oedipal father. It is in this area of illusion (generated by mother and child) that the external object Oedipal mother (and father) are nontraumatically discovered and the triangulated Oedipus complex begins to be elaborated.

The male Oedipus complex is built upon a foundation that is vulnerable to erosion. For the little boy, the external object mother bears an uncanny resemblance to the pre-Oedipal internal object mother. This in part derives from the fact that there is no change of love object as is the case in female Oedipal development. The little boy's intense attachment to—and his feeling of need for—the pre-Oedipal mother are powerful forces tending to keep him an infant and child forever. He cannot become a man in relation to a magical sorceress; he can only engage in the ultimately futile effort to become magical himself. One of the multiple functions of the primal scene phantasy is the use to which it is put by the little boy at the threshold of the Oedipus complex in his effort to find a solution to this dilemma. In one version of the primal scene phantasy that develops at this juncture, the little boy is the excluded observer of parental sexual intercourse while at the same time being a participant in it (through identification with each of his parents). In this relatively differentiated version of the primal scene phantasy the little boy creates a narrative in which there exists recognition of sexual and generational difference, a father who is phallically empowered (and empowering), and an external object mother who has ties to, but is not subsumed by, the omnipotent pre-Oedipal mother. The phantasy of the father's penis in the mother's vagina concretely represents the presence of thirdness that triangulates the formerly dyadic relationship that had existed between the little boy and the omnipotent pre-Oedipal mother. In this version of the primal scene phantasy, the little boy is becoming an interpreting subject (observer) who is sufficiently *outside* of the sexual act to be equated with neither the phallus, nor with an omnipotent form of female sexuality, nor with sexual excitement itself. And yet at the same time he is sufficiently "inside" of the phantasy to experience himself as phallically empowered in identification with the father (who is at first the father-in-mother).

The Initial Analytic Meeting

We shall not cease from exploration
And the end of all our exploring
Will be to arrive where we started
And know the place for the first time.

T. S. Eliot, "Little Gidding"

Psychoanalytic concepts and techniques, in order to retain their vitality, must again and again be discovered by the analyst as if for the first time. The analyst must allow himself to be freshly surprised by the ideas and phenomena that he takes most for granted. For example, he must be able to allow himself to be genuinely caught off guard by the pervasiveness of the influence of the unconscious mind, by the power of the transference, and by the intransigence of resistance — and to only retrospectively apply the familiar names to these freshly rediscovered phenomena. If the analyst allows himself to perpetually be the beginner that he is, it is sometimes possible to learn that which he thought he already knew. This chapter is a collection of thoughts addressed to myself (and other novices) on the subject of the opening of the analytic drama. I will make no attempt to be exhaustive since the topic touches upon almost every aspect of psychoanalytic theory and technique. My starting point for a discussion of the first analytic meeting is the idea that there is no difference between the analytic process in the first meeting and that in any other analytic meeting: the analyst in the initial meeting is no more or less an analyst, the analysand no more or less an analysand, the analysis no more or less an analysis than in any other meeting.

Creating Analytic Significance

Everything that the analyst does in the first face-to-face analytic session is intended as an invitation to the patient to consider the meaning of his experience. All that has been most obvious to the patient will no longer be treated as self-evident; rather, the familiar is to be wondered about, to be puzzled over, to be newly created in the analytic setting. The patient's thoughts and feelings, his past and present, have new significance, and therefore the patient himself takes on a form of significance that he has never held before. There is a particular form of significance generated in the analytic context that is unique to that setting. For the analysand, the consulting room is a profoundly quiet place as he realizes that he must find a voice with which to tell his story. This voice is the sound of his thoughts that he may never have heard before. (The analysand may find that he does not have a voice that feels like his own. This discovery may then serve as the starting point of the analysis.)

The analyst both speaks and refrains from speaking in a way that communicates the fact that he accepts the patient as he is without judgment; and yet at the same time it is understood by both patient and analyst that they are meeting together for the purpose of psychological change. The analyst attempts to understand why the patient is as he is and cannot change, and yet he implicitly asks the patient to give up his illness sufficiently to make use of the analysis. For example, the schizoid patient must enter into a relationship with the analyst in order to overcome his terror of even the most minimal involvement with other people; the obsessional patient, in order to get help with his endless ruminations, must give up his ruminations sufficiently to enter into an analytic dialogue; the hysterical patient must interrupt the drama that constitutes (and substitutes for) his life long enough to become an observer of that life, in addition to being an actor in it.

The analyst is the object of the patient's transference feelings even before the first meeting. In addition to viewing the analyst as a person trained to understand and (through some as yet unknown process) help the patient find relief from psychic pain, the analyst is also frequently experienced by the patient as the healing mother, the childhood transitional object, the wished-for Oedipal mother and father, and so on. With these hopes comes the fear of disappointment.

Just as the patient has a (phantasied) analyst before the first session, the analyst also has a patient (more accurately, he has many patients) in his own mind prior to the initial meeting. In other words, prior to meeting the patient, the analyst has drawn upon such elements as the

sound of the patient's voice on the telephone, the source
of the referral, and the analyst's relationships with his
current patients, as sources of conscious and unconscious
feelings about the patient that he will bring to the first
analytic meeting. In addition, there is regularly a feeling
of suspense connected with the anticipation of the initial
interview. Both patient and analyst are about to enter into
an interpersonal drama for which there are many scripts
already written (the analyst's and the patient's internal
dramas), and yet if the work is to be productive, a drama
never before imagined by either will have to be created.
Along with the sense of excitement, there is also an edge
of anxiety. For both analyst and patient, the danger
posed by the first meeting arises to a large extent from the
prospect of a fresh encounter with one's own inner world
and the internal world of another person. It is always
dangerous business to stir up the depths of the unconscious mind. This anxiety is regularly misrecognized by
therapists early in practice. It is treated as if it were a fear
that the patient will leave treatment; in fact the therapist
is afraid that the patient will stay.

A patient recently described to me with unusual
clarity a fragment of her train of thought prior to the first
meeting: "How much should I say in the beginning about
the things of which I am most afraid and ashamed? How
should I phrase it? I don't want him to think I am so
crazy, so deceitful, so selfish, so seductive, that working
with me will be experienced as so unpleasant that he will
soon find some excuse for getting rid of me. Is the
humiliation of revealing myself in this way worth it? Did
I make a mistake in deciding to see him? He was
disappointing to me when I spoke to him on the phone. I
wish he were older, more like a grandfather. He sounded
a little crazy: he didn't seem to know his own address. His

office is in a kind of decrepit neighborhood. I wonder if he's having trouble in his practice."

When a potential patient phones to inquire about working with me in therapy or analysis, I suggest that we find a time to meet for a consultation. I intentionally use the word *consultation* in order to make it clear that this meeting will not necessarily be the beginning of ongoing work for us together (despite the fact that I intend it to be an analytic experience regardless of what the outcome of the meeting might be). I do this because I cannot know ahead of time whether, after talking with the patient, I will feel that I can be of help to him and will want to work with him. Among the multiplicity of factors that go into making this determination is the question of whether I feel that I generally like the patient and feel some concern for and interest in him.

It is important that the analyst attempt in part to organize his thinking diagnostically in an effort to conceptualize the nature of the analytic work that the patient will require and the nature of the difficulties that the analytic pair is likely to encounter. However, with a few exceptions (such as drug- or alcohol-addicted patients, violently acting-out sociopaths, and severely organically damaged patients), I am generally open to working analytically with patients suffering from a wide range of psychological disturbances (cf. Boyer, 1971; Giovacchini, 1969, 1979; Ogden, 1982b, 1986). But it seems to me that one is claiming too much if one claims to be able to work with any patient who is interested in analysis. I believe that we do a patient a disservice if we agree to work with him when we are aware that we do not like him. It is sometimes said that the analyst ought to be able to analyze his negative countertransference and therefore should be able to work with any patient who is otherwise suitable for analytic work. In theory this may be true; however, in practice, I believe that the analytic task is difficult enough without attempting to build the analytic edifice upon a foundation of a powerful negative countertransference (or an intense negative transference). In my experience, this is so whether or not the analyst (or the patient) recognizes these transferences to be irrational. This caveat has seemed to me equally applicable to instances in which there are from the beginning very intense erotic transferences or countertransferences.

On the other hand, when speaking with a patient I do not refer to the initial meeting as an "evaluation period" or "assessment phase" since these designations seem to me to convey the idea that the patient is to be relatively passive in this enterprise. Such terms would misrepresent my understanding that the function of the first meeting centrally involves the initiation of the analytic process. The nature of the interaction of the first meeting is not simply that of one person evaluating another or even of two people evaluating each other. Rather, it is in my view an interaction in which two people attempt to generate analytic significance, including an understanding of the meanings of the decision-making process that is involved in the initial meeting. It is my intention in this meeting to facilitate the creation of an interaction that will constitute an analytic experience of some value to the patient, in that it will provide him with a sense of what it means to be in analysis.

Despite the fact that transference anxiety is extremely high in the period leading to the initial interview, I do not view it as the analyst's job to put the patient at ease in the first meeting. On the contrary, I believe that it is the analyst's task to help the patient not miss an important opportunity to recognize and understand something about the transference thoughts, feelings, and sensations with which he has been struggling.

Sustaining Psychological Strain in the Analytic Setting

As with all other analytic meetings, the initial hour begins in the waiting room. The patient is addressed as Dr., Mr., or Ms., and the analyst introduces himself in kind. The paradox inherent in this formal introduction is not lost to the patient: the analytic relationship is one of the most formal and at the same time one of the most intimate of human relationships. The formality is a reflection of respect for the analysand and for the analytic process. In addition, it is an expression of the fact that the analyst is not pretending to be, nor does he aspire to be, the analysand's friend. (We do not pay our friends to talk to us.) It is therefore made clear from the outset that the intimacy of the analytic relationship will be an intimacy in the context of formality.

Therapists early in their training often feel the impulse to "put the patient at ease" or "to act human" as they walk with the patient from the waiting room to the consulting room. For instance, a therapist attempting to ease the tension of the walk to the consulting room might say, "I hope you didn't have trouble finding a parking space. Parking is awful around here." To make such a comment is not a kind thing to do from the point of view of the analytic process. In fact, from the perspective being discussed in this chapter, such a therapist would be considered rather unkind in several ways. First, he has communicated to the patient his unconscious feeling that the patient is an infant who has trouble making his way in a hostile world, and also the fact that the therapist feels guiltily responsible for not making the patient's life less difficult. Such a comment immediately puts the patient into the analyst's debt and puts pressure on him to return the "kindness" — that is, to help the analyst avoid feelings of discomfort. There is also a hint in the therapist's comment that he is not confident that the therapy he will offer the patient is worth the trouble to which the patient is going.

Furthermore, this sort of comment is an act of theft: it robs the patient of the opportunity to introduce himself to the analyst in the way that he consciously and unconsciously chooses. The patient has available to him an infinite number of ways of beginning the analytic discourse. His choice of the way he will go about doing this will be repeated by no other analysand. One must not deprive him of his opportunity to write the opening lines of his own analytic drama by burdening him with the analyst's own unconscious contents before he even sets foot in the consulting room. (There will be plenty of time for that later as the analyst inevitably becomes an unwitting actor in the patient's unconscious phantasies.)

Finally, a comment of the type being discussed misleads the patient about the nature of the analytic experience. As analysts, we do not intend to relieve anxiety (our own or the patient's) through tension-reducing activity such as reassurances, gift-giving, and the like. Since maintaining psychological strain is not only something that we demand of ourselves, but also part of what we ask of the patient, it makes no sense to begin the analytic relationship with an effort at dissipating psychological strain. Whether or not the incident is ever spoken of again, the analysand unconsciously registers the fact that the analyst has granted himself license to handle his own anxiety by acting upon his countertransference feelings.

The patient brings to the first interview many questions and worries (usually unspoken) about what it means to be in analysis, what it means to be an analyst, and what it means to be an analysand. The analyst's attempts at answering these questions in the form of explanations of free association, the use of the couch, frequency of meetings, differences between psychotherapy and psychoanalysis, differences between "schools of psychoanalysis," and so on, are not only futile but invariably highly limiting of the patient's opportunity to present himself to the analyst in his own terms. As is illustrated by the following clinical vignette, the analyst's most eloquent explanation of what it means to be "in analysis" is to conduct himself as an analyst.

Mr. H., a 42-year-old television producer, explained in the initial session that he had come to see me because he felt intensely anxious and had "obsessional ideas" about dying, including fears of suffocating in his sleep and of being trapped and killed during an earthquake. The patient was also preoccupied by the thought that his 6-year-old daughter, who was mildly hearing-impaired, would "not be able to make it in the world." He said that he knew that each of his fears was overblown, but this knowledge did not diminish the intensity of his anxiety.

The patient said that he had been fearful from the time he was a small child. Mr. H.'s father, who was a college professor, was continually dissatisfied with the patient, and insisted on "helping him" with his homework each night. This inevitably ended with the father's shrieking at the son for his "incredible stupidity."

Mr. H. told me that his success at work seemed unreal to him. He felt as if he had to be continually preparing for the day when he would no longer be able to function. As a result, he hoarded every penny that he earned. He gave several examples of feeling dangerously depleted when he spent money. I then said that it seemed as if he was suggesting that the idea of paying for analysis would be frightening because it would mean giving up one of the few sources of protection that he felt he had. Mr. H. smiled and said that he had thought a great deal about this, and that the prospect of paying for analysis felt to him like a blood-letting in which there would be a race between his "cure" and his bleeding to death.

When I met Mr. H. in the waiting room for our second meeting, he was perspiring and seemed to have been waiting for me like a man anxiously awaiting some terribly important piece of news, perhaps a verdict. Immediately upon entering my consulting room, he walked briskly across the room and reached for the phone, saying, "I locked my keys in the car and so if it's all right, I'd like to call my wife to ask her to meet me here with a spare set of keys after our meeting." I said that I thought it must seem to him as if his life depended on his making the phone call, but I thought that he and I should talk about what it was that was happening between us before attempting to undo it. He sat down and said, "Actually, what just happened is kind of typical of me. I drove here with my lunch in the back seat of my car, and when I arrived I saw a sign in the parking garage that said, 'Leave keys in car.' I felt uneasy about leaving my lunch in an unlocked car. I had the thought that some-body might tamper with my lunch and so I didn't want to leave the car unlocked."

I said to Mr. H. that without realizing it he seemed

to have done both things he had intended to do: he had locked his lunch in the car so it would not be tampered with, and had left his keys in the car as the sign had directed. He told me that he had become very panicky when he realized that his keys were locked in his car and immediately thought of calling his wife from my office. He said that he had felt greatly relieved by this idea. I repeated his realization that he had thought of me as well as his wife at that moment. He said that was true, but that he had also thought of me earlier when he saw the sign which somehow seemed to have been put there by me.

Mr. H. explained that the request to use my phone was also characteristic of him. He said he was almost always afraid that people were angry at him, and he regularly reassured himself that people liked him by asking small favors of them. For example, he frequently borrowed change or a pencil from colleagues at work, or asked directions to a place when he already knew perfectly well how to get there.

He told me that he was certain that I already thought he was "a real jerk." (I assumed that there was a wish as well as a fear underlying this feeling, but I did not interrupt the patient at this point since he was in the midst of introducing me to the cast of characters constituting his internal object world.) Mr. H. went on at this point to tell me more about his parents. His father had died ten years earlier, but had lived his entire life as if he were at death's door. He had suffered from renal disease originating in childhood and was preoccupied with the fear of death. The patient said that as a child he had been frightened that his father would die when his father was yelling at him. Mr. H. told me that his father could at times be very kind and that the patient had loved him despite the fact that he had been frightened of him so much of the time.

I asked if the patient had expected that I would yell at him for locking his keys in the car and for asking to use my phone. He said that he thought he had had that feeling in a diffuse sort of way, but had not quite known why he was feeling so frightened while waiting in my waiting room. (It occurred to me that the patient may have been attempting to call his wife in an effort to get her to protect him from me [as his mother had protected him from his father] and to protect me from himself.)

In the course of the analytic work that followed, many layers of meaning of this transference enactment (referred to by the patient as the "telephone caper") came to light. One of these was the patient's wish to be treated as a helpless little boy, thus defending himself against his feelings of being a powerfully destructive person who had done great harm to his father and who would do harm to me. A second aspect of this transference enactment involved the wish to provoke me into acting in a manner similar to that of his father, wherein I would yell at him for his stupidity. In part, he was afraid that I would act in that way and was attempting to reassure himself that I would not. In another way, he found sensual pleasure in such intense scoldings. In addition, he felt relief at the prospect of being punished, since this is what he unconsciously felt he deserved for the crime he imagined he had committed in relation to his father (that is, provoking him to the point that he had made him sick and ultimately had killed him). Furthermore, he felt that his father had demonstrated love for him in the father's intense, controlling involvement. The patient unconsciously hoped to elicit from me this form of love in the anticipated scolding. Over the course of the analysis, the "telephone caper" served again and again as a symbol of the analytic process.

Cautionary Tales

In the initial interview I listen from the outset for the patient's "cautionary tales" — that is, the patient's unconscious explanations of why he feels that the analysis is a dangerous undertaking, and his reasons for feeling that the analysis is certain to fail.[1] To say this is to say nothing more than that I listen for (and attempt to put into words for myself and for the patient) the leading edge of transference anxiety. Whatever the nature of the analysand's disturbances, his anxieties will be given form in terms of the danger of entering into a relationship with the analyst. The patient unconsciously holds a fierce conviction (which he has no way of articulating) that his infantile and early childhood experience has taught him about the specific ways in which each of his object relationships will inevitably become painful, disappointing, overly stimulating, annihilating, lonely, unreliable, suffocating, overly sexualized, and so on. There is no reason for him to believe that the relationship into which he is about to enter will be any different. In this belief, the analysand is of course both correct and incorrect. He is correct in the sense that transferentially, his internal object world will inevitably become a living intersubjective drama on the analytic stage. He is incorrect to the extent that the analytic context will not be identical to the

---

[1]Ella Freeman Sharpe (1943) used the term *cautionary tales* to refer to phantasies serving the purpose of instinctual impulse control by means of unconscious self-warnings of bodily destruction. In this chapter, I use the term to refer to a more circumscribed and differently conceptualized set of phantasies: the patient's unconscious set of phantasies concerning the dangers of entering into the analytic relationship (McKee, 1969).

original psychological-interpersonal context within which his internal object world was created — that is, the context of infantile and childhood phantasy and object relations.

Everything that the analysand says (and does not say) in the first hours can be heard in the light of an unconscious warning to the analyst concerning the reasons why neither the analyst nor the patient should enter into this doomed and dangerous relationship. It must be emphasized that the patient feels that the analysis will endanger the analyst as well as himself, and that it is largely in an effort to protect the analyst that the patient balks at entering the relationship. The analyst, from this perspective, serves as the container for the patient's fears about beginning this relationship, as well as the container for the patient's hopes that internal change is possible and that pathological attachments to internal objects can be altered without sacrificing the life of the patient. The following account of an initial analytic meeting is an illustration of one such way in which patients unconsciously attempt to symbolize for themselves and for the analyst the dangers that they anticipate.

An analysand began his first meeting by describing his empty relationship with his wife and children, the boredom that he felt at work, and the lack of joy that he felt in his life in general. He said that he had been referred to me by his internist who thought analysis would be of benefit to him. Despite Mr. J.'s presentation of his feelings of desolation, I suspected that there were pleasures in his life that he felt he must keep secret both from himself and from me. I had the fantasy that Mr. J. was having an affair — perhaps with a woman, perhaps with music, art, or some other "passionate interest," perhaps with the memory of a childhood romance. This fantasy was not the product of intuition, but a response to something about the patient's presentation of himself. In retrospect, it is easier to see that this had been communicated to me by his choice of words, by his rhythm of speech, by his gait, by his facial expressions and so on. He behaved like a man with a secret. I surmised (but did not say to Mr. J.) that he unconsciously seemed to feel that analysis would contain forms of pleasure that he would have to keep well hidden. As a result, I anticipated that analysis would have a rather arid feeling to it (both for him and for me) for quite a long time.

The patient said that he felt convinced that he needed treatment, and that he knew that his wife and children would benefit if he were to get help. Nonetheless, he felt extremely guilty about spending money on analysis which could be spent in buying things that his whole family could enjoy. I said after some time had elapsed in the first hour that the patient seemed to feel that beginning analysis would be equivalent to having an affair. He told me how devoted he was to his wife and that he had never considered the idea of really having an affair. However, he said that it was strange that I had said what I had because earlier that week, for the first time, he had heard himself making a comment to his secretary that was sufficiently ambiguous as to have been construed as a proposition. She chose not to directly respond to the ambiguously proposed affair. He said that he had felt quite disturbed by this episode and had left work early for the first time in years.

In this instance, I elected to interpret an aspect of what I understood to be Mr. J.'s leading transference anxiety (that is, the most accessible unconscious/preconscious set of transference and resistance meanings). The internal drama that the patient seemed to be bringing to the analytic relationship was one in which there was an anticipation of passionate attachment and intense secretiveness. It was within this area of experience (the "affair") that I suspected that Mr. J. was afraid the analysis would become extremely painful and perhaps impossible to continue.

In the course of the succeeding several years of analysis the patient was able to make sense of these feelings in terms of a childhood relationship he had had with a nanny whom he had loved deeply; it was a love that he had unconsciously felt he had to keep secret from his mother. His feelings of anger and guilt, as well as his fear of becoming involved in similar impossible entanglements, had led to Mr. J.'s developing a character defense in which he remained rather detached in all sectors of his life. The idea that he was "only going through the motions" served important defensive functions in the initial stages of his analysis.

The Timing of Transference Interpretations

As a result of my interest in ideas developed in the British psychoanalytic dialogue, I have often been asked if it is true that Kleinians interpret the transference from the very beginning of the analysis. The question is always a puzzling one to me. It hardly seems surprising that one would attempt to talk with the patient about what it is about this new relationship (the analytic relationship) that is so frightening, exciting, disappointing, futile, and so on. Generally, the initial session does not feel complete to me unless the patient's anxiety in the transference has in some way been addressed. One does not have to be a Kleinian to talk with one's patient about one's current (and always tentative) understanding of what it is that is disturbing to the analysand about the initial meeting.[2]

The following is an illustration of a situation in which there was countertransference resistance to discussing transference anxiety in the initial meeting.

A 32-year-old man made a phone call to a therapist for the purpose of setting up a consultation. He told her in the course of asking for an appointment that he felt in danger of getting into disputes that would end up in his punching someone. Mr. N. said that he is a large man, that he speaks in a booming voice, and that people are often frightened by him even when he is not angry. He said that despite all this, he hoped that the therapist would not be afraid of him since he was not a dangerous person and had never attacked anybody.

When Mr. N. appeared for his initial meeting, the therapist was surprised to find that the patient was a man of average build who spoke in a pressured manner, but not a loud or bullying one. She learned that Mr. N. was a successful owner of a retail business. He had been born to a psychotic mother and was placed in a foster home just before his first birthday. Mr. N. had seen neither his mother nor his father since that time. After a succession of five foster home placements in a five-year period, he was finally adopted by a couple with whom he lived until he left home at 18 to join the army. During the course of his latency and adolescence, the patient's adoptive parents had become alcoholics.

---

[2]At the same time, clinical judgment must guide the analyst in every therapeutic situation. There are many instances in which the analyst senses that it is critical that he not be too "clever" (Winnicott, 1968, p. 86) or know too much, and therefore chooses to refrain from offering even the most tentative versions of what he thinks he understands (cf. Balint, 1968; Winnicott, 1971a,c).

The therapist (who had only recently completed her training) did not discuss with the patient his implicit, ambivalent warning that she would be well advised to have nothing to do with him. There seems to have been an unconscious belief on the part of the therapist that talking to Mr. N. about his fear of his destructiveness would make him more dangerous to her. There was also a denial of her own fear of the patient that left her unable to think about his warning. (Other therapists might have refused to even meet with this patient, thus engaging in a transference-countertransference enactment of the patient's experience of himself as a danger to both his internal and external objects. The patient, after all, had already — from the perspective of his unconscious psychic reality — caused his original mother to become psychotic, leading her to abandon him; had been so unlovable and perhaps dangerous as to have caused five sets of foster parents to refuse to keep him; and had driven his adoptive parents to alcoholism.)

The patient came to his next four weekly meetings in an increasingly agitated state. Several days after the fifth meeting, Mr. N. phoned the therapist saying that he had felt more and more anxious after each of his meetings with her and that it had become unbearable. He had therefore decided to discontinue therapy. The therapist suggested that Mr. N. come to another meeting in order to talk about these feelings.

It was at this point that the therapist sought consultation on the case. I suggested to her that the patient had indicated from the very outset that he was terrified that his anger (particularly in the maternal transference) would frighten and damage the therapist. The therapist's unconscious fear of the patient had led her to suggest once-a-week meetings with Mr. N. despite indirect indications from him that he felt he needed and could afford more intensive therapy. This unconscious decision on the part of the therapist to seek a safe distance from the patient had confirmed the patient's belief that the therapist would (with good reason) find him dangerous, and would eventually refuse to see him. It seemed to me that Mr. N. had telephoned the therapist in order to see whether she had been injured in the previous meeting and that he had been temporarily reassured by her asking him to come to his next meeting. I hypothesized that Mr. N. was in a rage at his (internal object) mother for being crazy and unable to love him and for having abandoned him. At the same time, he was terrified that it was his anger that had driven his mother crazy and had led her to abandon him.

Mr. N. began the meeting that followed the telephone call by asking the therapist, "How are you?" as they walked from the waiting room to the consulting room. Once in the consulting room, he said that his heart was pounding. The therapist suggested that Mr. N. was worried that he had scared or perhaps hurt her at the previous meeting and that this had been a concern of his from the very beginning. The patient calmed down considerably after this interpretation. The therapist later in the meeting suggested that since the patient felt such intense anxiety in response to each meeting, it might be useful to meet more frequently in order to discuss what it was that was frightening him. To the therapist's surprise, Mr. N. seemed receptive to this idea. In a sense, the beginning of the analytic dialogue had been postponed for six or seven meetings largely as a result of unanalyzed anxiety in the countertransference, which had led to the therapist's inability to think about or interpret the patient's transference anxiety.

Analytic Space

Entry into the analytic experience (beginning in the initial interview) involves the enlargement of the psychological space constituting the "matrix of the mind" (Ogden, 1986) in such a way that this space more or less comes to approximate the analytic space; thus, the analytic space becomes the space in which the patient thinks, feels, and lives. In a subtle way, the events making up the patient's experience in relation to his internal and external objects, the events making up his daily life and his responses to these events, come to be important to him insofar as they contribute to the analytic experience. Eventually, it is not the patient's individual psychological space but — to a large degree — the analytic space that constitutes the space in which the patient's unconscious internal drama is experienced. The evolution of this process includes, but is by no means limited to, that which is usually referred to as the elaboration of the transference neurosis and the transference psychosis.[4]

That which constitutes analytic space is individual to each analytic pair. Just as each mother learns (often to her surprise) that the process of creating a play space differs greatly with each of her children, the analyst must learn that the process of creating analytic space is different with each analysand (Goldberg, 1989). In the same

---

[4]From this perspective, the termination phase of an analysis is not simply a phase of resolution of conflicted unconscious transference meanings. As importantly, it is a period of the "contraction" of the analytic space such that the patient comes to experience *himself* as constituting the space within which he lives and within which the analytic process continues. If this does not occur, the prospect of the end of the analysis is experienced as tantamount to the loss of one's mind, or the loss of the space in which one feels alive.

way that each infant's unique character draws upon and brings to life specific aspects of the emotional potential of the mother, the analyst must allow himself to be created/ molded by his patient in reality as well as in phantasy. Since the infant has a role in creating his mother, no two infants ever have the same mother. Similarly, no two patients ever have the same analyst. The analyst experiences himself differently, and behaves in a subtly different manner, in each analysis. Moreover, this is not at all a static phenomenon: in the course of each analysis the analyst undergoes psychological change which in turn is reflected in the way he conducts the analysis.

More seriously disturbed patients may experience the analytic space as a vacuum which threatens to suck out of them their mental contents (which are concretely experienced as bodily parts or contents). One such patient began the first meeting by barraging me with an uninterrupted series of obscenities. Taken aback by the onslaught, I decided to allow the patient to have his say and to observe the impact that he was having on me. It became apparent that his barrage was far more anxious than it was hostile. After about five minutes, I said to him that I thought it was not easy for him to be there with me. He quieted down as I said this. I then told him that I thought he had emptied his garbage into me because he did not mind giving up a part of himself that he did not value. I said that I guessed he had more important things inside of him that he felt he needed to protect. Following this intervention, the patient was able to tell me more about himself, albeit in a psychotic way. I, in turn, discussed with him the little bit of what I thought I understood of what he was telling me. Almost all of what I said was addressed to the patient's fears about being with me.

Anxious Questioning

Analysands often pose direct questions in the initial meeting. A few of these I will answer directly. For example, I will in a "matter-of-course" way (Freud, 1931, p. 131) answer the patient's questions about my training or my fee. Most questions, however, I do not answer, including questions about whether I have a particular specialty, with which "school of psychoanalysis" I am associated, whether I see more men than women in my practice, whether I consider homosexuality to be an illness, and the like. These sorts of questions are treated as rather undisguised statements of the patient's phantasies about the specific ways in which I will fail to understand him, due to my own psychological difficulties, such as a fear of women or men, a fear of homosexuality or heterosexuality, a need to dominate or submit to others, and so on.

When a patient persistently asks question after question, I often say to him that it must feel too dangerous to wait to see what happens between us; that instead of waiting, the patient seems to be trying to sample the future through the answers to his questions, thereby short-circuiting the tension connected with waiting.

Very often the analysand uses questions in an attempt to get the analyst to fill the analytic space because the patient feels that his own internal contents are shameful, dangerous, worthless, and/or in need of protection from the analyst, or that there is nothing at all inside of him with which to occupy the analytic space. Other patients may quickly fall silent, thus inviting the analyst to fill the space with his (the analyst's) questions and therefore with the analyst's psychological organization, chain of associations, curiosity, and the like. Under such circumstances, I attempt to talk with the patient about the aspect of his anxiety that I think I understand. In so doing I make it clear that my understanding is tentative, and that in all likelihood it is quite lacking in many ways. In this way, I invite the patient to tell me which parts of what I have said seem true to him and which parts seem off the mark.

Creating a History

The question often arises as to whether one "takes a history" in the initial meeting. The very form of the question seems to me to have significance. I attempt not to "take" a history from a patient (by means of a series of questions), and instead make every effort to allow the patient to *give* me his conscious and unconscious versions of his history in his own way.[5] The patient has come to see the the analyst for help with psychological pain, the nature of which he (the patient) is often unable to accurately name. He must be afforded all the time and room that he needs to tell the analyst, in whatever way he has available to him, what he knows about himself. It is

---

[5]It is essential to keep in mind that a patient's history is not a static entity that is gradually unearthed; rather, it is an aspect of the patient's conscious and unconscious conception of himself that is in a continual state of evolution and flux. In a sense, the patient's history is continually being created and re-created in the course of the analysis. Moreover, it is by no means to be assumed that the patient has a history (that is, a sense of historicity) at the beginning of analysis. In other words, we cannot take for granted the idea that the patient has achieved a sense of continuity of self over time, such that his past feels as if it is connected to his experience of himself in the present.

important that the analyst not interfere with the patient's efforts by introducing an agenda of his own, by doing such things as collecting historical data, making treatment recommendations, or laying out the "ground rules" of analysis (cf. Freud, 1913; see also Shapiro, 1984).

In the course of the patient's telling the analyst, however indirectly, about the nature of his pain (and the ways he consciously and/or unconsciously expects this pain to become exacerbated in the course of analysis), his past experience will be articulated in two ways. First, to the extent that the patient tells the analyst about his understanding of the origins of his difficulties, he will be giving the analyst one form of historical data — that which the patient consciously conceives of as his past. Inevitably there will be gaps, vaguenesses, or complete omissions of large sectors of the patient's life experience. For example, a patient may omit any reference to a given family member, make no mention of his sexual experience, or be silent about everything that occurred prior to the current crisis or prior to his adolescence. Under such circumstances, when I feel that the patient has told me what he wants to and what he is able to, I may ask him if he has noticed his not mentioning, for example, anything about his father. (This is essentially a process of addressing the patient's relationship to his external and internal objects from the point of view of resistance; that is, from the point of view of the patient's conscious and unconscious object-related anxiety.)

As with any comment addressing resistance, it is not the information "behind" the resistance that is of central concern; the focus is on what it is that the patient is afraid will happen if he tells the analyst about a given aspect of his internal life, and about his ways of protecting himself against this danger. From this perspective, the act of "taking a history" (by means of direct inquiry) is a form of overriding the patient's resistances and thereby losing a good deal of what is most important to the analysis — for example, an understanding of who in the patient's internal object world would be betrayed, injured, killed, lost, made jealous, and so on, if the patient were to talk about his feelings about "the past"; or what sort of loss of control over the patient's relationships to his internal objects would be experienced in his giving up exclusive access to them.

The second form of personal history provided by the patient is data conveyed unconsciously in the form of the transference–countertransference experience. This is the patient's "living past," the set of object relations established in infancy and early childhood which has come to constitute the structure of the patient's mind, both as content and context of his psychological life. It is therefore this past that is of central analytic interest.

Of course, the two forms of history under discussion — the consciously symbolized past and the unconscious living past — are intimately intertwined. As the patient's internal object world is given intersubjective life in the transference–countertransference during analysis, both patient and analyst have an opportunity to directly experience the forms of attachment, hostility, jealousy, envy, and the like constituting the patient's internal object world. In the transference–countertransference, the past and the present converge as "old" contents are brought to life in a new context, the context of the analytic relationship.

Concluding Comments

The ideas that I have discussed in this chapter are simply that — ideas. They are not intended to be used as rules or guidelines, nor are they intended as a statement of how the initial analytic meeting should be conducted. At the same time, the thoughts discussed here are thoughts of a specific nature — they are psychoanalytic thoughts. This represents one of the dialectics constituting psychoanalytic technique: analytic technique is guided by a set of ideas that are roughly recognizable as forming a method or group of methods, with a set of principles that gives coherence to this group of methods. From the first meeting, analytic practice occurs between the poles of the predictable and the unpredictable, the disciplined and the spontaneous, the methodical and the intuitive.

Summary

The initial face-to-face analytic meeting is viewed as the beginning of the analytic process and not merely as a preparation for it. In the first meeting all that was familiar to the patient is no longer treated as self-evident. The analysand takes on a form of significance for himself that he has never held before. The analyst attempts to convey to the patient something of what it means to be in analysis, not by means of explanations of the analytic process, but by conducting himself as an analyst. To this end, psychological strain is not dissipated through reassurance, suggestion, transference or countertransference, acting out, and so on. All that the patient says (and does not say) in the initial meeting is understood as an unconscious warning to the analyst (and to the patient) concerning the reasons why the patient unconsciously feels that each of them would be well advised not to enter into this doomed and dangerous relationship. The analyst attempts to understand the patient's warnings in terms of transference anxiety and resistance.

8

Misrecognitions and the Fear of Not Knowing

The work of a group of British and French psychoanalytic thinkers, including Bion, Lacan, McDougall, Tustin, and Winnicott, has led me to understand certain psychological difficulties in terms of an unconscious fear of not knowing. What the individual is not able to know is what he feels, and therefore who, if anyone, he is. The patient regularly creates the illusion for himself (and secondarily for others) that he is able to generate thoughts and feelings, wishes and fears that feel like his own. Although this illusion constitutes an effective defense against the terror of not knowing what one feels or who one is, it further alienates the individual from himself. The illusion of knowing is achieved through the creation of a wide range of substitute formations that fill the "potential space" (Winnicott, 1971d) in which desire and fear, appetite and fullness, love and hate might otherwise come into being.

The "misrecognitions" that are used as defenses against the fear of not knowing represent a less extreme

195

form of alienation from affective experience than "alex-ithymia" (Nemiah, 1977), states of "non-experience" (Og-den, 1980, 1982b), and "disaffected" states (McDougall, 1984), wherein potential feelings and phantasies are foreclosed from the psychological sphere. It is also a less extreme psychological catastrophe than schizophrenic fragmentation wherein there is very little of a self capable of creating, shaping, and organizing the internal and external stimuli that ordinarily constitute experience. The patients I will be focusing upon have the capacity to generate a sense of self sufficiently integrated and suffi-ciently bounded to enable them to know that they do not know. That is, these are patients who are able to experi-ence the beginnings of feelings of confusion, emptiness, despair, and panic, as well as being able to mobilize defenses against these incipient feelings.

As will be discussed, in the course of an infant's development a sense of self evolves in the context of the management of need by the mother–infant pair. When the mother can satisfactorily tolerate the recognition of her own desires and fears, she is less afraid of the states of tension generated by her infant that are in the process of becoming feelings. When the mother is capable of tolerating the infant's tension over time, it is possible for her to respond to a given tension state as a quality of the infant's being alive.

A Theoretical Background

The development of the idea of misrecognitions of one's internal state is in a sense synonymous with the develop-ment of psychoanalytic theory. One of the cornerstones upon which Freud constructed his theory of psychological meanings is the idea that one knows more than he thinks he knows. The creation of psychological defenses can be understood as the organization of systematic misrecognitions (for example, it is not my anger that I fear, it is yours). Freud (1911b), in his discussion of the Schreber case, explored the idea that psychosis involves the misrecognition of one's internal state through its attribution to external objects.

It is beyond the scope of this chapter to review, or even list, the multitude of contributions to the question of psychological misrecognition and the defenses associated with it. In the following pages, however, I will briefly discuss a group of concepts developed by French and British psychoanalytic thinkers that have particular relevance to the ideas being developed in the present chapter.

Lacan (1948) believed that Freud in his later work "seems suddenly to fail to recognize the existence of everything that the ego neglects, scotomizes, misconstrues in the sensations" (p. 22). Lacan's (1953) understanding of the ego as the psychic agency of *méconnaissance* (misrecognition) derives from his conception of the place of the ego in relation both to language and to the imaginary and symbolic orders of experience. The realm of the imaginary is that of vital, unmediated, lived experience. In this realm, there is no space between oneself and one's experience. The acquisition of language provides the individual a means by which to mediate between the self as interpreting subject and one's lived experience. Since language and the chain of signifiers that constitute language predate each of us as individuals, the register of symbols that is made available to us through language has nothing to do with us as individuals. We do not create the symbols we use; we inherit them. As a result, language misrepresents the uniqueness of our own lived experience: "It [language] is susceptible to every alienation or lie, wilful or not, susceptible to all the distortions inscribed in the very principles of the 'symbolic,' conventional dimension of group life" (Lemaire, 1970, p. 57).

In becoming a subject capable of using symbols to interpret our experience, rather than simply being trapped in our own lived sensory experience, we exchange one form of imprisonment for another. We acquire human subjectivity at the cost of becoming profoundly alienated from our immediate sensory experience (which is now distorted and misrepresented by the symbols we use to name it). In this way, we unwittingly engage in a form of self-deception, creating for ourselves the illusion that we express our experience in language, while we are in fact, according to Lacan, misnaming and becoming alienated from our experience.

Joyce McDougall, an important contributor to the French psychoanalytic dialogue, has discussed her work with patients who seemed "totally unaware [and thus kept the analyst unaware] of the nature of their affective reactions" (1984, p. 388). She understands this phenomenon as a dispersal of potential affect into a variety of addictive actions including drug abuse, compulsive sexuality, bulimia, "accidental" injuries, and interpersonal crises. Such addictive activities are understood as compulsive ways of defending against psychotic-level anxieties. As the defensive use of the affect-dispersing action becomes overtaxed, the individual engages in psychosomatic foreclosure and "psychosomatic misinterpretation" (McDougall, 1989) of events in the psychological sphere. Under such circumstances, what might have become a symbolically represented affective experience is relegated to the domain of the physiologic and becomes disconnected from the realm of conscious and unconscious mental representations.

Such a conception of the destruction not only of psychological meaning, but of the apparatuses generating psychological meaning, represents an elaboration of the work of Wilfred Bion. Bion (1962) suggests that in schizophrenia (and to lesser degrees in all personality organizations), there is a defensive attack on the psychological processes by which meaning is attached to experience. This represents a superordinate defense in which psychological pain is warded off, not simply through defensive rearrangements of meaning (such as projection and displacement) and interpersonal evacuation of endangered and endangering internal objects (projective identification); in addition, there is an attack on the psychological processes by which meaning itself is created. The outcome is a state of "non-experience" (Ogden, 1980, 1982b) in which the individual lives partly in a state of psychological deadness—that is, there are sectors of his personality in which even unconscious meanings and affects cease to be elaborated.

In the course of his writing, Winnicott developed the concept of a "potential space" in which self-experience is created and recognized (Winnicott, 1971d; see also Ogden, 1985b, 1986). Potential space is the space in which the object is simultaneously created and discovered. That is, in this space, the object is simultaneously a subjective object (an object omnipotently created) and an object objectively perceived (an object experienced as lying outside of the realm of one's omnipotence). The question of which is the case—is the object created or discovered—never arises (Winnicott, 1951). This question is simply not a part of the emotional vocabulary of this area of experience. We do not move through, or grow out of, this state of mind. It is not a developmental phase; rather, it is a psychological space between reality and phantasy that is maintained throughout one's life. It is the space in which playing occurs; it is the space in which we are creative in the most ordinary sense of the word; it is the space in which we experience ourselves as alive and as the authors of our bodily sensations, thoughts, feelings, and perceptions. In the absence of the capacity to generate potential space, one relies on defensive substitutes for the experience of being alive (such as the development of a False Self personality organization [Winnicott, 1960b]).

The "fear of breakdown" described by Winnicott (1974) represents a form of failure to generate experience in which the patient is terrified of experiencing for the first time a catastrophe that has already occurred. The very early environmental failure that constituted the catastrophe could not be experienced at the time that it occurred, because there was not yet a self capable of experiencing it — that is, capable of elaborating the event psychologically, and of integrating it. As a result, the patient forever fearfully awaits his own psychological breakdown.

In this chapter I address a specific facet of the phenomenon of the alienation from, and destruction of, experience. My focus is on the anxiety associated with the dim awareness that one does not know what one feels and therefore does not know who one is. In this psychological state, the individual has not foreclosed experience psychosomatically or failed to psychologically elaborate early experience, nor has he entered into a state of "non-experience." The patients discussed here have often attempted, but have not entirely succeeded in, warding off the anxiety of not knowing by means of addictive actions. The form of experience that I am interested in here is one in which the individual is sufficiently capable of generating a space in which to live such that he is capable of knowing that he does not know; he never entirely frees himself of this terror, much as he unconsciously attempts to lure himself and the analyst into mistaking his systematic misrecognitions for genuine self-experience. Such experience is universal and is manifested in a wide variety of forms that reflect the individual's personality organization.

A Developmental Perspective

At the outset, it is the infant's relationship with his mother that is the matrix within which psychological tension is sustained over time sufficiently for meanings to be created and desire and fear to be generated. For example, what will become hunger is initially only a physiologic event (a certain blood sugar level registered by groups of neurons in the brain). This biological event becomes the experience of hunger and desire (appetite) in the context of the mother's conscious and unconscious response to the infant: her holding, touching, nursing, and rocking the infant and engaging in other activities that reflect her understanding of (her conscious and unconscious resonance with) him (Winnicott, 1967b). Such understandings and attendant activities are the outcome of a crucial psychological function provided by the mother: the psychological process by which the mother attempts to respond to her infant in a way that "correctly names" (or gives shape to) the infant's internal state.

The work of Bick (1968), Meltzer (1975), and Tustin (1981, 1986) has afforded analytic theory a way of conceptualizing the earliest organization of experience into sensation-dominated forms including autistic shapes ("felt shapes" [Tustin, 1984]) and autistic objects (Tustin, 1980). In the development of "normal autism" (what I have termed the elaboration of the *autistic-contiguous position* [see Chapters 2 and 3]), the infant in the context of the mother–infant relationship achieves the earliest sense of boundedness, the sense of having (being) a place (more specifically, a surface) where one's experience occurs and where a sense of order and containment is generated.

In the earliest mother–infant relationship, the mother must be capable of immersing herself in the infant's sensory world as she allows herself to de-integrate into relative shapelessness. This represents the sensory level of primitive empathy. The mother allows her identity as a person and as a mother to "become liquid" (Seale, 1987) in a way that parallels the internal state of the infant. This "de-integration" (Fordham, 1977) is not experienced by the mother as disintegration when she is able to create for herself a generative dialectical tension between the shapeless and the formed, the primitive and the mature, the mysterious and the familiar, the act of becoming a mother for the first time and the experience of having "been here before" (in her identification with facets of her experience with her own mother). In this way, the mother helps the infant give shape, boundedness, rhythm, edgedness, hardness, softness, and so on to his experience.

The mother and infant must attempt to sustain the strain of the very inexact, trial-and-error means by which each attempts to "get to know" the other. The mother's efforts at understanding, comforting, and in other ways providing for and interacting with her infant are inevitably narcissistically wounding to the mother since she will often feel at a loss to know what it is her baby needs and whether it is within the power of her personality to provide it even if she somehow could discover what he "wants." Winnicott's (1974) use of the word *agonies* to refer to infantile anxieties applies equally to the pain of the mother's experience of not knowing.

The Structuralization of Misrecognition

The early relationship that is of central interest in the analytic setting is not that of mother and infant, but that of the internal object mother and the internal object infant. This internal object relationship is manifested in the transference–countertransference phenomena that constitute the analytic drama. A mother–infant relationship is never directly observable in the analytic setting even when the patient is a mother describing current experience with her child. Instead, what we observe, and in part experience, in analysis is a reflection of internal object relations (our own and the patient's, and the interplay between the two). Therefore, when I speak of the internal relationship between mother and infant, it must be borne in mind that the patient is both mother and infant. This is so because an internal object relationship consists of a relationship between two unconscious aspects of the patient, one identified with the self and the other identified with the object in the original relationship (Ogden, 1983). Regardless of how fully autonomous an internal object may seem to the patient, the internal object can have no life of its own aside from that deriving from the aspect of the self involved in this identification. In what follows I describe a set of pathological internal mother–infant relationships in which the patient is both mother and infant, both the mis-namer and the mis-named, both the confused and the confusing.

The (internal object) mother may defend against the feeling of not knowing by utilizing obsessive-compulsive defenses, for example, by relying on rigidly scheduled (symbolic) feedings of the (internal object) infant. In this way, the mother (in this internal object relationship) invokes an impersonal external order (the clock) to misname hunger. The infant is responded to as if he were sated every four hours and as if he were not hungry between the scheduled feedings. Such misnaming generates confusion in the infant as well as a sense that hunger is an externally generated event. In the extreme this mode of defense against not knowing becomes a persecutory authoritarian substitution of the mother's absolute knowledge for the infant's potential to generate his own thoughts, feelings, and sensations.

Mothers enacting this sort of internal object relationship in their actual relationships to their own children are often "psychologically minded" and offer verbal interpretations of their children's unconscious feeling states. For example, a mother being seen in analysis informed her 7-year-old child that even though he claimed to be doing the best job that he could in learning to read, the truth of the matter was that he was angry at her and was doing a poor job of it because he knew precisely how to drive her crazy. Such "interpretations" may be partially accurate (due to the universality of such unconscious feelings as anger, jealousy, and envy in a mother–child relationship); but such comments predominantly have the effect of misnaming the child's internal state. The effect of such interpretation is the creation in the child of a feeling that he has no idea how he "really feels" and that only his mother has the capacity to know this. This patient's behavior in relation to her child represented an enactment of an internal object relationship derived from her own experience with a mother who had used fundamentalist religious dogma in the misrecognition of the patient's childhood feeling states. When such a relationship becomes established in the patient's internal object world, the role of this type of internal object mother is then projected onto the analyst. As a result, the patient comes to experience the analytic setting as an extremely dangerous, authoritarian one wherein the analyst will certainly tear apart the patient's character structure (including his conscious experience of himself) and "interpret" the shameful truth regarding the patient's unconscious thoughts and feelings.

The analyst may unwittingly be induced (as an unconscious participant in the patient's projective identification) to enact the role of such an authoritarian internal object mother (cf. Ogden, 1982b). Under such circumstances the analyst may find himself interpreting more "actively" and "deeply" than is his usual practice. He may come to view the analysis as bogged down, and to despair of the patient's ever arriving at meaningful insight. The analyst may rationalize that he needs to use a more didactic approach with the patient in order to demonstrate to him what it means "to think reflectively and in depth." Alternatively, the analyst may feel moved to pursue a line of analytic thinking espoused by his "school of psychoanalysis," or based upon an idea about which he has recently read. Reliance upon analytic ideology represents a common method of warding off the analyst's anxiety of not knowing.

Balint (1968) has suggested that the Kleinian technique of "consistent interpretation" represents a countertransference acting out of the role of an omniscient internal object. From the perspective of the ideas being explored in the present chapter, the analyst's unconscious identification with the omniscient internal object mother represents a form of defense against the anxiety of not knowing what it is the patient is experiencing. (Obviously, this is so whether or not the analyst is a Kleinian.) The patient's internal version of an early object relationship is in this way being replicated in the analytic setting, and unless analyzed in the countertransference and in the transference, this will reinforce the patient's unconscious conviction that it is necessary to utilize omnipotent substitute formations in the face of confusion about what he is experiencing and who he is.

Analytic candidates and other trainees frequently utilize this type of unconscious identification with an omnipotent internal object (such as an idealized version of one's own analyst). This identification serves as a defense against the anxiety that the candidate does not feel like an analyst when with his patients. Searles (1987) has described his own experience during his psychiatric residency, where he would "prop himself up" when talking with his patients by authoritatively offering them interpretations given to him only hours earlier by his analyst. Decades later, he became aware that he had experienced his own analyst (more accurately his own internal object analyst) as similarly propped up and filled with self-doubt. This deeper level of insight reflects the way in which the omniscient internal object serves as a substitute formation obscuring an underlying confusion about who one is and who the object is.

Patients may also enact the role of the omniscient internal object mother, by doing such things as controllingly interpreting the analyst's shifting in his chair as a reflection of his anxiety, sexual excitement, anger, or the like. When consistently subjected to this form of "interpretation" (that is indistinguishable from accusation), the analyst may unconsciously identify with the internal object infant (within the patient) who is exposed to continual misnaming of his internal state. Anxiety arising in the analyst under such circumstances may lead him into a form of countertransference acting out in which he attempts to "assist the patient in reality testing" by denying to the patient that he (the analyst) is feeling or acting in accord with the patient's interpretations.

A second form of defense against the fear of not knowing how to make sense of the feeling state of the internal object infant is the unconscious effort on the part of the patient to act as if he knows what the internal object infant is experiencing. In this way he creates a substitute formation for the feeling of being at a complete loss to make use of his capacities for understanding and responding to the internal object infant. Reliance on such a set of defenses may result in a rather stereotypic form of self-knowledge. A mother while in analysis described her attempts at being a mother by imitating the mothers portrayed in books and on television, by imitating her friends who had children, and by imitating the analyst's treatment of her. She attended every PTA and cub scout function, arranged for swimming, tennis, and music lessons, painstakingly baked pumpkin pies at Thanksgiving and mince pies at Christmas, and so on. The schizophrenic child of another such mother told his mother, "You've been just like a mother to me." Such mothers are "just like" mothers, but do not experience themselves (nor are they experienced by their children) as being mothers. The self-esteem of such mothers is brittle, and these women often collapse into depression or schizoid withdrawal as they become emotionally ex-

hausted in their efforts at imitating a psychological state
from which they feel utterly alienated.

A 30-year-old psychologist, Dr. M., in the course of
his analysis generated a transference–countertransference externalization of the form of internal object relationship just described. During the first two years of
work, I frequently questioned the value of the analysis
despite the fact that all seemed to be proceeding well. In
the third year, the patient began to wryly refer to me as
"the perfect analyst." He described how he was the envy
of all his colleagues for his unusual good fortune in
having the opportunity to work with me. Only recently
had he begun to become aware of his strong belief that he
and I were colluding in an effort to hide our awareness of
my shallowness and extreme emotional detachment. Dr.
M. presented a dream in which he had graduated from
college but was completely illiterate. In the dream, the
patient was unable to work because he could not read and
was unable to go back to school for fear of shaming his
teachers.

This dream represented Dr. M.'s emerging feeling
(that had been the unconscious context for the entire
analysis) that he and I were merely going through the
motions of analysis. Eventually he would have to pretend
to be "cured," which would mean that he would live in
absolute isolation without hope of ever genuinely feeling
a connection with anyone. In this case, the internal object
relationship that was recreated in the transference–countertransference involved the defensive use of an illusion
of perfection (the reliance on form as a replacement for
content) as a substitute for the real work of analyst and
patient awkwardly and imprecisely attempting to talk to
one another.

A third form of defense against the pain of feeling utterly confused about that which the internal object infant is experiencing is pathological projective identification. In this process one "knows" the other by "in phantasy" occupying the other with one's own thoughts, feelings, and sensations, and in this way short-circuiting the problem of the externality (and unpredictability) of the other. Under such circumstances, a mother (enacting an internal drama in relation to her own infant) may decide to allow her infant to cry for hours on end because she "knows" that the infant has such tyrannical strivings (the mother's own projected feelings about herself) that it is essential that she not be bullied by this baby Hitler. Under such circumstances the mother is not only defending herself against the destructive power of her own tyrannical internal object infant by locating these feelings in the actual infant (and at the same time maintaining an unconscious connection with this part of her internal object world); in addition, she is allaying the anxiety of not knowing by experiencing the actual infant as the fully known and predictable internal object for which she has a long-standing, clearly defined plan of defensive action.

In a sense, transference in general can be viewed as serving the function of making known the unknown object. Transference is a name we give to the illusion that the unknown object is already known: each new object relationship is cast in the image of past object relations with which one is already familiar. As a result, no encounter is experienced as entirely new. Transference provides the illusion that one has already been there before. Without this illusion, we would feel intolerably naked and unprepared in the face of experience with a new person.

Misrecognition of Affect: A Clinical Illustration

Mrs. R., a 42-year-old woman who had been in analysis
for almost three years, punctuated each meeting with
efforts to cajole, trick, plead, and in other ways coerce me
into "giving [her] something specific" in the form of
advice or insight. She hoped that when she left my office
she would be able to take with her what I gave her during
the meeting, and apply it to her life outside the analysis.
When I was silent for an entire session, the meeting was
considered wasted since "nothing had happened." Mrs.
R. responded with an intense display of emotion to any
disruption of analytic routine. If I were a few minutes
late in beginning the hour, she would either cry quietly or
remain angrily silent for the first ten to fifteen minutes of
the hour. She would then tell me that my being late could
only mean that I did not give a damn about her.
Consistent efforts at analyzing the content and intensity
of Mrs. R.'s reactions were made. She related this current
set of feelings to her childhood experience of waiting for
what had seemed like hours for her mother (a college
professor) while she spoke with students after class.
However, there reached a point when the material did not
become any richer as the patient repeatedly returned to
the image of angrily waiting for her mother. I found
myself becoming increasingly annoyed and was aware of
fantasies of making sadistic comments as the patient cried
in response to my informing her of a vacation break or a
rare change in the time of a given appointment.

In a session at the end of the third year of analysis,
I was three or four minutes late in beginning the session.
Mrs. R. was visibly upset when I met her in the waiting
room. In what had become her customary pattern, the
patient lay down on the couch, folded her arms across her

chest and was silent for about ten minutes. She finally said that she did not know why she continued in analysis with me. I must hate her, otherwise I would not treat her in such a callous manner. I asked her if she were really feeling at that moment that my lateness had reflected the fact that I hated her. She reflexively said, "Yes," but it was apparent that the question had taken her by surprise. After a few minutes, she said that in fact my lateness had not bothered her even though she had behaved as if it had. She said that in retrospect her recent reactions to me seemed to her to have been a little like play-acting, although she had not had that sense of things until I asked the question that I did today. I suggested that by acting as if she had felt crushed by my lateness, she obscured for herself the feeling that she did not know how she felt about it.

Over the succeeding year, as the analysis took on an increasing feeling of authenticity, it was possible to identify a plethora of forms of defense against the anxiety connected with the feeling of not knowing. The patient recognized that she had been unable to progress in her efforts to become an opera singer because she had from the beginning of her training bypassed various fundamentals of technique. She could create an initial impression of being a very accomplished singer, but this could not be sustained. The inability to "begin at the beginning" in her vocal training and to tolerate the tension of not knowing had severely interfered with Mrs. R.'s ability to learn. She had felt it necessary to create the illusion of being very advanced from the outset. Mrs. R. also became aware that it was extremely difficult for her to accurately identify her sensory experience, for example, to know whether she was anxious or in physical pain, in what part of her body the pain was arising, whether a given sensation reflected sexual excitement or a need to urinate, whether she was hungry or lonely, and so on.

The analysis then centered on Mrs. R.'s fear of the "spaces" in the analytic hour that had formerly been filled by what she referred to as her "play-acting" or by her pleading with me to give her something that she could take with her from the session. During the period of work in which these matters were being discussed, Mrs. R. began a session by saying that since she did not want to overdramatize, nor did she want to throw a temper tantrum, she was having trouble knowing what to say. Later in the same meeting the patient reported the following dream: she was in the office of a dentist who removed two of her molar teeth. She had not known he was going to do this, but had the feeling that she had somehow agreed to have it done. When he showed her the teeth, they looked perfect — they were perfectly shaped and had gleaming white enamel "like something you'd see in a storybook." She thought it strange that they did not have roots. The extraction had not been painful, and afterward, instead of pain, there was simply a strange feeling of empty spaces at the back of her mouth. The holes that were left in the gums rapidly closed over by themselves and did not require stitches. In making her associations, Mrs. R. was able to understand that the two teeth had represented two ways of behaving that she felt she was giving up in the analysis: the overdramatization and the temper tantrums. She said that like the teeth, these ways of being seemed to be losses that left a weird space. Moreover, this loss was a loss of something that did not seem to be quite real — like "storybook teeth without roots." This dream represented the beginnings of a phase of the analysis in which the patient was able to become gradually less reliant on misrecognition as a defense against the experience of not knowing.[1] These misrecognitions had filled the potential space in which inchoate desires and fears might have evolved into feelings that could be felt and named.[2]

Misrecognition as a Dimension of Eating Disorders

Patients with a wide range of eating disorders including anorexia nervosa and bulimia regularly report that their overeating or refusal to eat has nothing whatever to do with the experience of appetite. These patients are rarely able to generate an emotional/physiologic state that they can correctly recognize as an appetite for food. The psychological difficulty underlying the inability of these patients to generate appetite affects their capacity to generate almost every form of desire, including sexual desire, desire to learn, desire to work, desire to be with other people, and desire to be alone.

In the course of my work with patients suffering

---

[1] There are of course conflicted sexual and aggressive meanings suggested by the manifest content of this dream. However, it was necessary to analyze the patient's experience of not knowing what she was experiencing, before it became possible to analyze the conflictual content of that experience.

[2] It is characteristic of the analytic process that each insight (recognition) immediately becomes the next resistance (misrecognition). The patient's awareness of and understanding of the experience of not knowing is no exception to this principle. Invariably, as the analysand recognizes his warded-off state of not knowing, the feeling of confusion itself is utilized in the service of defending against that which the patient consciously and unconsciously knows, but does not wish to know.

from eating disorders, it has made increasing sense to me to think of many of these patients as suffering from a disorder of the recognition of desire. An important aspect of the experience of such a patient is his unconscious fear that he does not know what he desires. This leads him to ward off the panic associated with such awareness by behaving as if it is food that is desired. The patient may then obsessionally (usually ritualistically) eat and yet he never feels full since what has been taken in is not a response to a desire for food. Rather, the eating represents an attempt to use food *as if* that is what had been desired when in fact the individual does not know what it is to feel desire. In one such case an adolescent girl, in a state of extreme anxiety bordering on panic, consumed several loaves of bread and two cooked chickens. This resulted in gangrenous changes in her stomach because of the compromise of her blood supply, caused by over-distention of the gastric walls. Surgical removal of two thirds of her stomach was required. She had told her mother over the course of the preceding week that everything appeared colorless. The mother had responded by saying that it was natural to feel gray in the autumn, that everybody does.

      This adolescent, in her frantic eating, was not attempting to meet a need or to fulfill a desire; the problem was that she could not create a psychological space in which either need or desire could be generated. The patient therefore felt, to a large degree, as if she already were psychologically dead and it was this feeling that had led to her state of panic. Paradoxically, the patient was desperately eating in an attempt to create the feeling of hunger. More accurately, she was eating in order to create the illusion that she could feel hunger, which would serve as evidence that she was alive.

The early relationship between this patient and her mother seems to have been characterized by the same fear of recognition of the internal state of the patient that was reflected in the mother's comment about the universality of feelings of grayness — of melancholy — in the autumn. The bits of meaning that the patient had managed to attach to her own experience (in this case, the experience of colorless, lifeless depression) were stripped of meaning in the interaction with her mother (cf. Bion, 1962). The beginnings of meaning, generated in an internal psychological space, were transformed into a universal and therefore impersonal truth. This had had the effect of obliterating not only the bits of meaning that had been created, but more importantly, the internal psychological space that the patient had tenuously achieved.

Psychological Change in the Area of Recognition and Misrecognition

The following is an excerpt from the analysis of a 46-year-old computer scientist who began treatment not knowing why he had come for therapy (but seeming at the same time unaware of his not knowing). During the initial face-to-face interviews prior to his beginning to use the couch, Dr. L. described situations in which he felt anxious, such as while waiting to be assigned a table in a restaurant and before making business phone calls. The explanations the patient offered for his anxiety in these situations were formulae extracted almost verbatim from his extensive reading of popular self-help books.

By the time he turned 40, Dr. L. was internationally known and had amassed a large fortune as a result of his innovations in the area of computer technology. Even though the vast bulk of his money was now invested very conservatively, he experienced both his financial situation and his status in his field as extremely precarious. These fears led him to devote himself with ever-increasing intensity to his work. Only after several months of analysis did he say that he awoke every night in a state of extreme anxiety. He supposed he was anxious about his work, but he was not sure since he was unable to remember his dreams.

It is beyond the scope of this chapter to describe the analytic work underlying the psychological changes that ensued. My intention here is simply to illustrate the nature of psychological change in the area of the creation and recognition of desire. The following description of a dream presented by Dr. L. at the beginning of the third year of analysis is an illustration of such change.

I was standing in front of a large house and could see through the windows that the paint on the ceiling was cracking as a result of water that had leaked in from the roof. To my surprise, the old man who owned the house came out and asked me to come in and talk. He asked me if I knew who he was. I didn't and I told him that. The old man thanked me for being truthful. He told me who he was. . . . I can't remember what his name was. He told me he was going to die in two weeks and would like to give all of his money to me. I said that I didn't want the money. He took me into the next room, which was lined with fine old books and very beautiful antique furniture. He offered me the house and everything in it. I again said that I didn't want it.

I told him that I could get the water damage fixed. The old man said that the peeling paint was part of the house as he knew it and he didn't want it changed. I told him it could damage the house. The old man was very calm and explained that he had lived a happy life and that he would be dead in two weeks and so it didn't matter.

Dr. L. said that he woke up from this dream feeling a profound sense of contentment that he associated with memories of his maternal grandfather. Dr. L. recalled how his grandfather at the age of 85 had loved his garden, planting seeds for flowers one day, seeds for lettuce the next, seeds for other flowers the next, and so on. One day when the patient was about 6 years old he said to his grandfather, who was then planting flower seeds, "Grandpa, you planted that same row with carrot seeds yesterday." The patient's grandfather laughed and said, "Bobby, you don't understand. The point is the planting, not the growing."

The dream about the unfamiliar old man and the house, and the associations to this dream, represented a layering of alterations of what had previously been misrecognitions of affect. Dr. L. said that it had been "cleansing" to experience himself in the dream as a person who talked in language that "cut to the bone" in contrast to the "bullshit" with which he felt he usually filled his life. "I didn't know who the old man was and I simply said so. I felt a glimmer of temptation to accept his money and all of his stuff, but I really didn't want his money. Ordinarily, I would have thought that what I wanted was his money. I can see myself acting in a way that would have made him think that that's what I was after.[3] Actually, I just liked being with him. The old man and I offered one another things the other didn't want or have any use for. What meant so much to me was the way we explained ourselves to each other. I could feel all the tension in me subside when the old man said that he had lived in the house as it was and didn't want it changed."

Over the course of the meeting, the dream was understood to be a representation of the way Dr. L. wished that he and I could talk together. In the dream the patient had felt momentarily freed from his usual isolation that resulted from layer upon layer of misnamings and misrecognitions of his own internal state and that of the other.[4] The defensive internal misrecognitions had made it impossible for him to feel that he understood anything of what he felt toward other people and what they felt toward him. These misrecognitions had left the patient feeling alone and disconnected from a self (and the other) that he only dimly knew.

In the course of the succeeding months of analysis,

---

[3]It had taken me most of the first year of the analysis to become aware of the way Dr. L. unconsciously attempted to lure me into misrecognitions of his internal state by repeatedly mislabeling them, giving me misleading pictures of himself and of his relationships, leaving out important details, leading me to believe that he understood what was going on in an interpersonal situation when he did not, and the like.

[4]If the individual is unable to know what he feels, he is equally at a loss to know what it is that the other is experiencing. This is simply another way of stating that in the internal object relationship under discussion, the individual is both internal object mother and internal object infant, both misrecognized and misrecognizing. The outcome is a feeling of alienation from the other experienced by both the self and the object component of the internal object relationship.

Dr. L. became increasingly able to understand why he had come to see me in the first place and why he was continuing in analysis. Although he had been unaware of it at the time, the anxiety that he had experienced in going into restaurants and before making business phone calls had in part reflected an anticipation of the painful confusion and loneliness that he would feel in talking to people. He unconsciously expected that once again there would be only the illusion of two people talking to one another.

Dr. L. gradually related the set of feelings just discussed to a persistent childhood feeling of isolation. He had felt that his parents operated according to a logic that he could not fathom. In the course of analysis, Dr. L. was able to re-experience and articulate this powerful, but heretofore wholly unrecognized, set of background childhood feelings. The patient, in discussing the events of his current life, would return again and again to such statements as, "What kind of sense does that make?" "That doesn't add up. Why can't anyone see that?" "What kind of bullshit is this?" "Doesn't anyone have any common sense?" Such feelings were increasingly experienced in the transference, for example in relation to my policy of billing the patient for missed appointments. These feelings of outrage served an important defensive function: it was necessary for the patient to feel that he knew better than anyone else "what the story was." This served to obscure the patient's feeling of being utterly confused and disconnected from a firmly grounded sense of what he was feeling, what he wanted, or why he wanted it—and, most basically, what it meant in a visceral sense to experience (and name) desires and fears that felt like his own.

As the analysis went on, the patient increasingly

came to experience me as disturbingly insubstantial and
infinitely malleable. Dr. L. felt quite alone during the
sessions and said that attempting to have a relationship
with me was like "trying to build a house on a foundation
of Jello." He became preoccupied with the feeling that he
had no idea who I was. The patient engendered in me (by
means of what I eventually understood as a projective
identification) a sense of detachment that I have rarely
experienced with a patient. The couch concretely felt as if
it were located at a very great distance from my chair. At
these times I found it extremely difficult to focus on what
Dr. L. was saying. The patient's sense of isolation in the
relationship with me was gradually understood in terms
of his internal relationship with a schizoid mother who
"gave the appearance of being there until you realized
that she was unable to think."

Summary

In this chapter, I have discussed a set of unconscious,
pathological internal object relations in which misrecognitions of affect play a central role. These internal
object relations timelessly perpetuate the infant's subjective experience of the mother's difficulty in recognizing
and responding to the infant's internal state. Internal
object relationships are understood to involve a relationship between two unconscious aspects of the ego, one
identified with the self and the other identified with the
object of the original object relationship. Accordingly, in
the internal object relationship under discussion, the
patient is both mother and infant, both misrecognized
and misrecognizing. In the context of this internal relationship, the patient experiences anxiety, alienation, and

despair in connection with the feeling of not knowing what it is that he feels or who, if anyone, he is.

Substitute formations are utilized to create the illusion that the individual knows what he feels. Examples of such substitute formations include obsessional, authoritarian, as-if, False Self, and projective identificatory forms of control over one's internal and external objects. While these substitute formations help to ward off the feeling of not knowing, they also have the effect of filling the potential space in which feeling states (that are experienced as one's own) might arise.

In the analytic setting, internal object relations are externalized and, through the medium of the transference–countertransference, are given intersubjective life. Clinical illustrations have been presented of analytic work addressing the anxiety of not knowing one's internal state, and the defenses serving to ward off this anxiety.

References

Anthony, J. (1958). An experimental approach to the psycho-pathology of childhood: autism. *British Journal of Medical Psychology* 31:211–225.

Anzieu, D. (1970). Skin ego. In *Psychoanalysis in France,* pp. 17–32. New York: International Universities Press, 1980.

Applegarth, A. (1985). A reconsideration of the Oedipal phase in the female. Presented at the meeting of the American Psychoanalytic Association, Denver, May.

Balint, M. (1955). Friendly expanses — horrid empty spaces. *International Journal of Psycho-Analysis* 36:225–241.

_____ (1968). *The Basic Fault.* London: Tavistock.

Bibring, E. (1947). The so-called English School of psycho-analysis. *Psychoanalytic Quarterly* 16:69–93.

Bick, E. (1968). The experience of the skin in early object relations. *International Journal of Psycho-Analysis* 49:484–486.

_____ (1986). Further considerations on the function of the skin in early object relations. *British Journal of Psychotherapy* 2:292–299.

Bion, W. R. (1957). Differentiation of the psychotic from the non-psychotic personalities. In *Second Thoughts,* pp. 43–64. New York: Jason Aronson, 1967.

_____ (1959a). *Experiences in Groups.* New York: Basic Books.

_____ (1959b). Attacks on linking. *International Journal of Psycho-Analysis* 40:308–315.

_____ (1962). *Learning from Experience.* New York: Basic Books.

_____ (1963). *Elements of Psycho-Analysis.* London: Heinemann.

Bollas, C. (1979). The transformational object. *International Journal of Psycho-Analysis* 60:97–108.

Borges, J. L. (1960). Borges and I. In *Labyrinths,* pp. 246–247. New York: New Directions, 1964.

Bower, T. G. R. (1977). The object in the world of the infant. *Scientific American* 225:30–48.

Boyer, L. B. (1971). Psychoanalytic technique in the treatment of characterological and schizophrenic disorders. *International Journal of Psycho-Analysis* 52:67–86.

_____ (1983). *The Regressed Patient.* New York: Jason Aronson.

_____ (1986). Personal communication.

_____ (1987). Countertransference and technique in working with the regressed patient: further remarks. In *Master Clinicians on Treating the Regressed Patient,* ed. L. B. Boyer and P. L. Giovacchini. Northvale, NJ: Jason Aronson, 1989.

Boyer, L. B., and Giovacchini, P. L. (1967). *Psychoanalytic Treatment of Schizophrenic, Borderline and Characterological Disorders.* New York: Jason Aronson.

Brazelton, T. B. (1981). *On Becoming a Family: The Growth of Attachment.* New York: Delta/Seymour Lawrence.

Chasseguet-Smirgel, J. (1964). Feminine guilt and the Oedipus complex. In *Female Sexuality,* ed. J. Chasseguet-Smirgel, pp. 94–134. Ann Arbor: University of Michigan Press, 1970.

_____ (1984a). The archaic matrix of the Oedipus complex. In *Sexuality and Mind. The Role of the Father and the Mother in the Psyche,* pp. 74–91. New York: New York University Press, 1986.

_____ (1984b). *Creativity and Perversion.* New York: W. W. Norton.

Chodorow, N. (1978). *The Reproduction of Mothering: Psychoanal-*

ysis and the Sociology of Gender. Berkeley: University of California Press.

Chomsky, N. (1957). *Syntactic Structures.* The Hague: Mouton.

——— (1968). *Language and Mind.* New York: Harcourt, Brace and World.

Eigen, M. (1985). Toward Bion's starting point: between catastrophe and faith. *International Journal of Psycho-Analysis* 66:321–330.

Eimas, P. (1975). Speech perception in early infancy. In *Infant Perception: From Sensation to Cognition,* vol. 2, ed. L. B. Cohen and P. Salapatek, pp. 193–228. New York: Academic Press.

Eliot, T. S. (1950). Letter to Helen Gardner. In *The Art of T. S. Eliot,* ed. H. Gardner, p. 57. New York: E. P. Dutton.

Fairbairn, W. R. D. (1940). Schizoid factors in the personality. In *Psychoanalytic Studies of the Personality,* pp. 3–27. Boston: Routledge and Kegan Paul, 1952.

——— (1941). A revised psychopathology of the psychoses and psychoneuroses. In *Psychoanalytic Studies of the Personality,* pp. 28–58. Boston: Routledge and Kegan Paul, 1952.

——— (1943). The repression and the return of bad objects (with special reference to the "war neuroses"). In *Psychoanalytic Studies of the Personality,* pp. 59–81. Boston: Routledge and Kegan Paul, 1952.

——— (1944). Endopsychic structure considered in terms of object-relationships. In *Psychoanalytic Studies of the Personality,* pp. 82–136. Boston: Routledge and Kegan Paul, 1952.

——— (1946). Object-relationships and dynamic structure. In *Psychoanalytic Studies of the Personality,* pp. 137–151. Boston: Routledge and Kegan Paul, 1952.

——— (1952). *Psychoanalytic Studies of the Personality.* London: Routledge and Kegan Paul.

Fenichel, O. (1945). *The Psychoanalytic Theory of Neurosis.* New York: W. W. Norton.

Fordham, M. (1977). *Autism and the Self.* London: Heinemann.

Freud, S. (1897). Extracts from the Fliess papers, Letter 71. *Standard Edition* 1:263–266.

—— (1905). Three essays on the theory of sexuality. *Standard Edition* 7:125–248.

—— (1910). A special type of object choice made by men. *Standard Edition* 11:163–176.

—— (1911a). Formulations on the two principles of mental functioning. *Standard Edition* 12:213–226.

—— (1911b). Psycho-analytic notes on an autobiographical account of a case of paranoia (dementia paranoides). *Standard Edition* 12:3–82.

—— (1913). On beginning the treatment. *Standard Edition* 12:121–144.

—— (1916–17). Introductory lectures on psycho-analysis XXIII: The paths to the formation of symptoms. *Standard Edition* 16:358–377.

—— (1921). Group psychology and the analysis of the ego. *Standard Edition* 18:67–143.

—— (1923). The ego and the id. *Standard Edition* 19:3–66.

—— (1925). Some psychical consequences of the anatomical distinction between the sexes. *Standard Edition* 19:248–258.

—— (1931). Female sexuality. *Standard Edition* 21:225–243.

—— (1933). New introductory lectures, XXXIII: Femininity. *Standard Edition* 22:112–135.

Gaddini, E. (1969). On imitation. *International Journal of Psycho-Analysis* 50:475–484.

—— (1987). Notes on the mind–body question. *International Journal of Psycho-Analysis* 68:315–330.

Gaddini, R. (1978). Transitional object origins and the psychosomatic symptom. In *Between Reality and Fantasy*, ed. S. E. Grolnick, L. Barkin, and W. Muensterberger, pp. 109–131. New York: Jason Aronson.

—— (1987). Early care and the roots of internalization. *International Review of Psycho-Analysis* 14:321–334.

Gaddini, R., and Gaddini, E. (1959). Rumination in infancy.

In *Dynamic Psychopathology in Childhood,* ed. L. Jessner and E. Pavenstedt, pp. 166–185. New York: Grune & Stratton.

Galenson, E., and Roiphe, H. (1974). The emergence of genital awareness during the second year of life. In *Sex Differences in Behavior,* ed. R. Friedman, R. Richart, and R. Vandeivides, pp. 223–231. New York: Wiley.

Giovacchini, P. L. (1969). The influence of interpretation upon schizophrenic patients. *International Journal of Psycho-Analysis* 50:179–186.

_____ (1979). *Treatment of Primitive Mental States.* New York: Jason Aronson.

Goldberg, P. (1989). Actively seeking the holding environment. *Contemporary Psychoanalysis* 25:448–476

Green, A. (1975). The analyst, symbolization, and absence in the analytic setting. (On changes in analytic practice and analytic experience). *International Journal of Psycho-Analysis* 56:1–22.

_____ (1983). The dead mother. In *On Private Madness,* pp. 142–173. New York: International Universities Press, 1986.

Grotstein, J. (1978). Inner Space: its dimensions and its coordinates. *International Journal of Psycho-Analysis* 59:55–61.

_____ (1981). *Splitting and Projective Identification.* New York: Jason Aronson.

_____ (1983). A proposed revision of the psychoanalytic concept of primitive mental states: II. The borderline syndrome — Section I. Disorders of autistic safety and symbiotic relatedness. *Contemporary Psychoanalysis* 19:570–604.

_____ (1985). A proposed revision of the psychoanalytic concept of the death instinct. *Yearbook of Psychoanalysis and Psychotherapy* 1:299–326. Hillsdale, NJ: New Concept Press.

_____ (1987). Schizophrenia as a disorder of self-regulation and interactional regulation. Presented at the Boyer

House Foundation Conference: The Regressed Patient, San Francisco, March 21.

Guntrip, H. (1961). *Personality Structure and Human Interaction.* New York: International Universities Press.

⸺ (1969). *Schizoid Phenomena, Object-Relations and the Self.* New York: International Universities Press.

Habermas, J. (1968). *Knowledge and Human Interests.* Trans., J. Shapiro. Boston: Beacon Press, 1971.

Hegel, G. W. F. (1807). *Phenomenology of Spirit.* Trans., A. B. Miller. London: Oxford University Press, 1977.

Heimann, P. (1971). Re-evaluation of the Oedipus complex — the early stages. *International Journal of Psycho-Analysis* 33:84–92.

Horney, K. (1926). The flight from womanhood: the masculinity complex in women as viewed by men and by women. In *Feminine Psychology,* pp. 54–70. New York: W. W. Norton, 1967.

Isaacs, S. (1952). The nature and function of phantasy. In *Developments in Psycho-Analysis,* ed. M. Klein, P. Heimann, S. Isaacs, and J. Rivière, pp. 67–121. London: Hogarth Press.

Jacobson, E. (1964). *The Self and the Object World.* New York: International Universities Press.

Jones, E. (1935). Early female sexuality. *International Journal of Psycho-Analysis* 16:263–273.

Kanner, L. (1944). Early infantile autism. *Journal of Pediatrics* 25:211–217.

Kernberg, O. (1976). *Object Relations Theory and Clinical Psychoanalysis.* New York: Jason Aronson.

Klein, M. (1928). Early stages of the Oedipus conflict. *International Journal of Psycho-Analysis* 9:167–180.

⸺ (1935). A contribution to the psychogenesis of manic-depressive states. In *Contributions to Psycho-Analysis, 1921–1945,* pp. 282–311. London: Hogarth Press.

⸺ (1946). Notes on some schizoid mechanisms. In *Envy and Gratitude and Other Works, 1946–1963,* pp. 1–24. New York: Delacorte, 1975.

_____ (1948). On the theory of anxiety and guilt. In *Envy and Gratitude and Other Works, 1946-1963,* pp. 25-42. New York: Delacorte, 1975.

_____ (1952a). Mutual influences in the development of ego and id. In *Envy and Gratitude and Other Works, 1946-1963,* pp. 57-60. New York: Delacorte, 1975.

_____ (1952b). Some theoretical conclusions regarding the emotional life of the infant. In *Envy and Gratitude and Other Works, 1946-1963,* pp. 61-93. New York: Delacorte, 1975.

_____ (1955). On identification. In *Envy and Gratitude and Other Works, 1946-1963,* pp. 141-175. New York: Delacorte, 1975.

_____ (1957). Envy and gratitude. In *Envy and Gratitude and Other Works, 1946-1963,* pp. 176-234. New York: Delacorte, 1975.

_____ (1958). On the development of mental functioning. In *Envy and Gratitude and Other Works, 1946-1963,* pp. 236-246. New York: Delacorte, 1975.

_____ (1975). *Envy and Gratitude and Other Works, 1946-1963.* New York: Delacorte.

Klein, S. (1980). Autistic phenomena in neurotic patients. *International Journal of Psycho-Analysis* 61:395-401.

Kohut, H. (1971). *The Analysis of the Self.* New York: International Universities Press.

Kojève, A. (1934-1935). *Introduction to the Reading of Hegel.* Trans., J. H. Nichols, Jr. Ithaca, NY: Cornell University Press, 1969.

Lacan, J. (1948). Aggressivity in psychoanalysis. In *Écrits,* pp. 8-29. New York: W. W. Norton, 1977.

_____ (1953). The function and field of speech and language in psychoanalysis. In *Écrits,* pp. 30-113. New York: W. W. Norton, 1977.

_____ (1956-1957). Les formations de l'inconscient. (Seminars summarized by J.-B. Pontalis.) *Bulletin de Psychologie.*

_____ (1958). The signification of the phallus. In *Écrits,* pp. 281-291. New York: W. W. Norton, 1977.

Laplanche, J., and Pontalis, J.-B. (1967). *The Language of Psycho-Analysis.* Trans. D. Nicholson-Smith. New York: W. W. Norton, 1973.

Lemaire, A. (1970). *Jacques Lacan.* Trans. D. Macey. Boston: Routledge and Kegan Paul.

Leonard, M. (1966). Fathers and daughters: the significance of "fathering" in the psychosexual development of the girl. *International Journal of Psycho-Analysis* 47:325–334.

Lewin, B. (1950). *The Psychoanalysis of Elation.* New York: The Psychoanalytic Quarterly Press.

Little, M. (1958). On delusional transference (transference psychosis). *International Journal of Psycho-Analysis* 39: 134–138.

Loewald, H. (1979). The waning of the Oedipus complex. In *Papers on Psychoanalysis,* pp. 384–404. New Haven: Yale University Press.

Mahler, M. (1952). On childhood psychoses and schizophrenia: autistic and symbiotic infantile psychoses. *Psychoanalytic Study of the Child* 7:286–305.

———— (1968). *On Human Symbiosis and the Vicissitudes of Individuation.* Vol. 1. New York: International Universities Press.

Mayer, E. (1985). "Everybody must be just like me": observations on female castration anxiety. *International Journal of Psycho-Analysis* 66:331–348.

McDougall, J. (1974). The psychosoma and the psychoanalytic process. *International Review of Psycho-Analysis* 1:437–459.

———— (1980). The primal scene and the perverse scenario. In *A Plea for a Measure of Abnormality,* pp. 53–86. New York: International Universities Press.

———— (1982). The staging of the irrepresentable: "A child is being eaten." In *Theaters of the Mind: Illusion and Truth on the Psychoanalytic Stage,* pp. 81–106. New York: Basic Books, 1985.

———— (1984). The "dis-affected" patient: reflections on affect pathology. *Psychoanalytic Quarterly* 53:386–409.

_____ (1986). Identifications, neoneeds, and neosexualities. *International Journal of Psycho-Analysis* 67:19–32.

_____ (1989). Personal communication.

McKee, B. (1969). Personal communication.

Meltzer, D. (1975). Adhesive identification. *Contemporary Psychoanalysis* 11:289–310.

_____ (1986). Discussion of Esther Bick's paper "Further considerations on the function of the skin in early object relations." *British Journal of Psychotherapy* 2:300–301.

Meltzer, D., Bremner, J., Hoxter, S., Weddell, D., and Wittenberg, I. (1975). *Explorations in Autism.* Perthshire, Scotland: Clunie Press.

Milner, M. (1969). *The Hands of the Living God.* London: Hogarth Press.

Nemiah, J. (1977). Alexithymia: a theoretical statement. *Psychotherapy and Psychosomatics* 28:199–206.

Ogden, T. (1979). On projective identification. *International Journal of Psycho-Analysis* 60:357–373.

_____ (1980). On the nature of schizophrenic conflict. *International Journal of Psycho-Analysis* 61:513–533.

_____ (1982a). Treatment of the schizophrenic state of non-experience. In *Technical Factors in the Treatment of the Severely Disturbed Patient,* ed. P. L. Giovacchini and L. B. Boyer, pp. 217–260. New York: Jason Aronson.

_____ (1982b). *Projective Identification and Psychotherapeutic Technique.* New York: Jason Aronson.

_____ (1983). The concept of internal object relations. *International Journal of Psycho-Analysis* 64:181–198.

_____ (1984). Instinct, phantasy and psychological deep structure: a reinterpretation of aspects of the work of Melanie Klein. *Contemporary Psychoanalysis* 20:500–525.

_____ (1985a). The mother, the infant and the matrix: interpretations of aspects of the work of Donald Winnicott. *Contemporary Psychoanalysis* 21:346–371.

_____ (1985b). On potential space. *International Journal of Psycho-Analysis* 66:129–141.

_____ (1986). *The Matrix of the Mind: Object Relations and the*

Psychoanalytic Dialogue. Northvale, NJ: Jason Aronson.

Parens, H., Pollock, L., Stern, J., and Kramer, S. (1976). On the girl's entry into the Oedipus complex. *Journal of the American Psychoanalytic Association* 24 (suppl): 79–107.

Rosenfeld, D. (1984). Hypochondrias, somatic delusion and body scheme in psychoanalytic practice. *International Journal of Psycho-Analysis* 65:377–388.

Sachs, L. (1977). Two cases of Oedipal conflict beginning at eighteen months. *International Journal of Psycho-Analysis* 58:57–66.

Sander, L. (1964). Adaptive relations in early mother–child interactions. *Journal of the American Academy of Child Psychiatry* 3:231–264.

Schafer, R. (1968). *Aspects of Internalization.* New York: International Universities Press.

—— (1974). Problems in Freud's psychology of women. *Journal of the American Psychoanalytic Association* 22:459–485.

Seale, A. (1987). Personal communication.

Searles, H. (1959). Oedipal love in the countertransference. *International Journal of Psycho-Analysis* 40:180–190.

—— (1960). *The Nonhuman Environment.* New York: International Universities Press.

—— (1963). Transference psychosis in the psychotherapy of chronic schizophrenia. In *Collected Papers on Schizophrenia and Related Subjects,* pp. 654–716. New York: International Universities Press, 1965.

—— (1966). *Collected Papers on Schizophrenia and Related Subjects.* New York: International Universities Press.

—— (1979). Jealousy involving an internal object. In *Advances in Psychotherapy of the Borderline Patient,* ed. J. Le Boit and A. Capponi, pp. 347–404. New York: Jason Aronson.

—— (1982). Some aspects of separation and loss in psychoanalytic therapy with borderline patients. In *My Work with Borderline Patients,* pp. 287–326. Northvale, NJ: Jason Aronson, 1986.

—— (1987). Concerning unconscious identifications. In

Master Clinicians on Treating the Regressed Patient, ed. L. B. Boyer and P. L. Giovacchini. Northvale, NJ: Jason Aronson, 1989.

Segal, H. (1957). Notes on symbol formation. *International Journal of Psycho-Analysis* 38:391–397.

Shapiro, S. (1984). The initial assessment of the patient: a psychoanalytic approach. *International Review of Psycho-Analysis* 11:11–25.

Sharpe, E. (1943). Cautionary tales. In *Collected Papers on Psycho-Analysis,* pp. 170–180. London: Hogarth Press, 1950.

Spitz, R. (1965). *The First Year of Life.* New York: International Universities Press.

Stern, D. (1977). *The First Relationship: Infant and Mother.* Cambridge: Harvard University Press.

_____ (1983). The early development of schemas of self, other and "self with other." In *Reflections on Self Psychology,* ed. J. Lichtenberg and S. Kaplan, pp. 49–84. Hillsdale, NJ: Analytic Press.

_____ (1985). *The Interpersonal World of the Infant.* New York: Basic Books.

Stoller, R. (1973). Symbiosis anxiety and the development of masculinity. Presented at the Fourth Annual Margaret S. Mahler Symposium, Philadelphia, May.

Trevarthan, C. (1979). Communication and cooperation in early infancy: a description of primary intersubjectivity. In *Before Speech,* ed. M. Bellowa. Cambridge: Cambridge University Press.

Tustin, F. (1972). *Autism and Childhood Psychosis.* London: Hogarth Press.

_____ (1980). Autistic objects. *International Review of Psycho-Analysis* 7:27–40.

_____ (1981). *Autistic States in Children.* Boston: Routledge and Kegan Paul.

_____ (1984). Autistic shapes. *International Review of Psycho-Analysis* 279–290.

——— (1986). *Autistic Barriers in Neurotic Patients.* New Haven: Yale University Press, 1987.

Winnicott, D. W. (1949). *The Child, the Family and the Outside World.* Baltimore: Penguin Books, 1964.

——— (1951). Transitional objects and transitional phenomena. In *Playing and Reality,* pp. 1–25. New York: Basic Books, 1971.

——— (1952). Psychoses and child care. In *Through Paediatrics to Psycho-Analysis,* pp. 219–228. New York: Basic Books, 1975.

——— (1954). The depressive position in normal development. In *Through Paediatrics to Psycho-Analysis,* pp. 262–277. New York: Basic Books, 1975.

——— (1956). Primary maternal preoccupation. In *Through Paediatrics to Psycho-Analysis,* pp. 300–305. New York: Basic Books, 1975.

——— (1958). The capacity to be alone. In *The Maturational Processes and the Facilitating Environment,* pp. 29–36. New York: International Universities Press, 1965.

——— (1960a). The theory of the parent–infant relationship. In *The Maturational Processes and the Facilitating Environment,* pp. 37–55. New York: International Universities Press, 1965.

——— (1960b). Ego distortion in terms of true and false self. In *The Maturational Processes and the Facilitating Environment,* pp. 140–152. New York: International Universities Press, 1965.

——— (1962). Ego integration in child development. In *The Maturational Processes and the Facilitating Environment,* pp. 56–63. New York: International Universities Press, 1965.

——— (1963a). The development of the capacity for concern. In *The Maturational Processes and the Facilitating Environment,* pp. 73–82. New York: International Universities Press, 1965.

——— (1963b). Communicating and not communicating leading to a study of certain opposites. In *The Maturational*

Processes and the Facilitating Environment, pp. 179–192. New York: International Universities Press, 1965.

———— (1965). Letter to Michael Fordham, 15 July 1965. In *The Spontaneous Gesture: Selected Letters of D. W. Winnicott,* ed. F. R. Rodman, pp. 150–151. Cambridge: Harvard University Press, 1987.

———— (1967a). The location of cultural experience. In *Playing and Reality,* pp. 95–103. New York: Basic Books, 1971.

———— (1967b). Mirror-role of mother and family in child development. In *Playing and Reality,* pp. 111–118. New York: Basic Books, 1971.

———— (1968). The use of an object and relating through identifications. In *Playing and Reality,* pp. 86–94. New York: Basic Books, 1971.

———— (1971a). *Playing and Reality.* New York: Basic Books.

———— (1971b). Playing: a theoretical statement. In *Playing and Reality,* pp. 38–52. New York: Basic Books.

———— (1971c). Playing: creative activity and the search for the self. In *Playing and Reality,* pp. 53–64. New York: Basic Books.

———— (1971d). The place where we live. In *Playing and Reality,* pp. 104–110. New York: Basic Books.

———— (1974). Fear of breakdown. *International Review of Psycho-Analysis* 1:103–107.

Index